Ignore Everybody

IGNORE EVERYBODY

And 39 Other Keys to Creativity

Hugh MacLeod

PORTFOLIO

PORTFOLIO

Published by the Penguin Group

Penguin Group (USA) Inc., 375 Hudson Street, New York, New York 10014, U.S.A. ▪ Penguin Group (Canada), 90 Eglinton Avenue East, Suite 700, Toronto, Ontario, Canada M4P 2Y3 (a division of Pearson Penguin Canada Inc.) ▪ Penguin Books Ltd, 80 Strand, London WC2R 0RL, England ▪ Penguin Ireland, 25 St. Stephen's Green, Dublin 2, Ireland (a division of Penguin Books Ltd) ▪ Penguin Books Australia Ltd, 250 Camberwell Road, Camberwell, Victoria 3124, Australia (a division of Pearson Australia Group Pty Ltd) ▪ Penguin Books India Pvt Ltd, 11 Community Centre, Panchsheel Park, New Delhi – 110 017, India ▪ Penguin Group (NZ), 67 Apollo Drive, Rosedale, North Shore 0632, New Zealand (a division of Pearson New Zealand Ltd) ▪ Penguin Books (South Africa) (Pty) Ltd, 24 Sturdee Avenue, Rosebank, Johannesburg 2196, South Africa

Penguin Books Ltd, Registered Offices:
80 Strand, London WC2R 0RL, England

First published in 2009 by Portfolio,
a member of Penguin Group (USA) Inc.

10 9 8 7 6 5 4 3 2 1

Selections from this book first appeared on the author's Web site, www.gapingvoid.com.

LIBRARY OF CONGRESS CATALOGING IN PUBLICATION DATA
MacLeod, Hugh, 1965–
Ignore everybody : and 39 other keys to creativity / Hugh MacLeod.
    p.   cm.
Includes index.
ISBN 978-1-59184-259-0
1. Business cards. 2. Advertising cards. 3. Creativity in advertising.
4. Macleod, Hugh, 1965– I. Title.
HF5851.M33 2009
650.1—dc22   2008054678

Printed in the United States of America
Set in AG Schoolbook
Designed by Daniel Lagin

This book is dedicated to my nephews and nieces—
lots of love from Uncle Hugh!

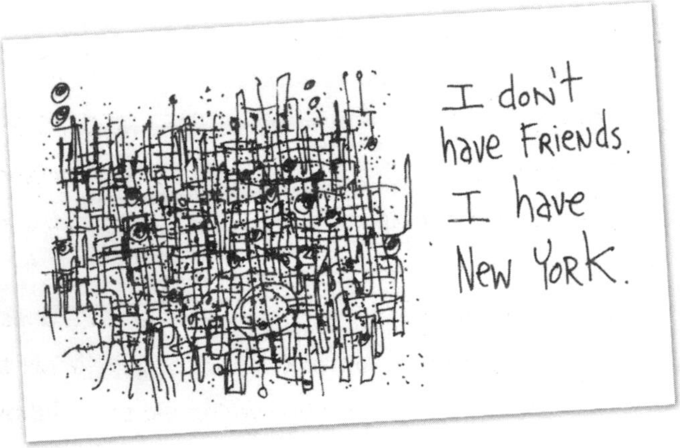
I don't have Friends. I have New York.

Preface

WHEN I FIRST LIVED IN MANHATTAN IN DECEM-
ber 1997, I got into the habit of doodling on the backs of business
cards, just to give me something to do while sitting at the bar.
The habit stuck.

All I had when I first got to New York were two suitcases, a
couple of cardboard boxes full of stuff, a reservation at the
YMCA, and a ten-day freelance copywriting gig at a Midtown
advertising agency.

My life for the next couple of weeks was going to work, walking
around the city, and staggering back to the YMCA once the bars
closed. Lots of alcohol and coffee shops. Lots of weird people.
Being hit five times a day by this strange desire to laugh, sing, and
cry simultaneously. At times like these, there's a lot to be said for
an art form that fits easily inside your coat pocket.

The freelance gig turned into a permanent job, and I stayed
in town for the next two years. The first month in New York for a

newcomer has this certain amazing magic about it that is inde-
scribable. Incandescent lucidity. However long you stay in New
York, you pretty much spend the rest of your time there trying to
recapture that feeling. Chasing the Manhattan Dragon. Somehow the little drawings on the backs of business cards managed
to capture this—the intensity, the fleeting nature, the everlasting
song of New York.

This has been my predominant cartoon format for over ten
years. The originals are drawn on either business cards, or bris-
tol board cut to the same size, i.e. 3.5 inches by 2 inches. I use
mostly a Rotring 0.3mm Rapidograph pen with jet-black India
ink. Occasionally I'll use other things—pencil, watercolor, ball-
point, tablet PC—but not often.

In 2001, then living in the UK, I started a blog, gapingvoid
.com, where I began publishing my "business-card cartoons"
online. In 2004 I published a series of blog posts that collec-
tively went on to become "How to Be Creative," which formed
the basis of the book you're reading now. In the meantime I've
had many adventures, as a cartoonist, a blogger, and a mar-
keter. I now reside in far West Texas, miles away from any big
city. To get the whole story of my trials, travels, and, well, life, go
check out my blog and give it a read.

"How to Be Creative," an earlier incarnation of *Ignore Everybody*, has so far been downloaded over a million times. For both
creative and commercial reasons, I've made some changes from
the original online document—adding more chapters and car-

toons to it, and replacing certain potty-mouth words with something more palatable. But part of the deal I made with the publisher going into this project was that I was totally unwilling to alter the spirit of the original blog posts just to see the book appear in print. Happily, they wanted it to remain pretty much as is, within reason. For that I remain very grateful to them.

I can't decide what I want to be: A millionaire or an Artist.
Can't you just compromise? Become a millionaire artist or something....

Contents

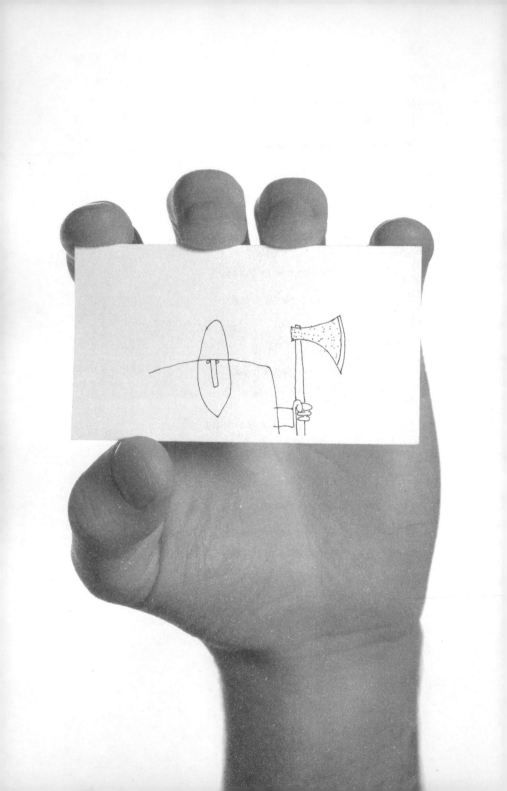

Ignore Everybody

He came to the Big City in order to get his Life together. His Life had other plans

1. **Ignore everybody.**

The more original your idea is, the less good advice other people will be able to give you. When I first started with the cartoon-on-back-of-bizcard format, people thought I was nuts. Why wasn't I trying to do something that was easier for markets to digest, like cutie-pie greeting cards or whatever?

YOU DON'T KNOW IF YOUR IDEA IS ANY GOOD the moment it's created. Neither does anyone else. The most you can hope for is a strong gut feeling that it is. And trusting your feelings is not as easy as the optimists say it is. There's a reason why feelings scare us—because what they tell us and what the rest of the world tells us are often two different things.

And asking close friends never works quite as well as you hope, either. It's not that they deliberately want to be unhelpful. It's just that they don't know your world one millionth as well as

1

you know your world, no matter how hard they try, no matter how hard you try to explain.

Plus a big idea will change you. Your friends may love you, but they may not want you to change. If you change, then their dynamic with you also changes. They might prefer things the way they are, that's how they love you—the way you are, not the way you may become.

Ergo, they might not have any incentive to see you change. If so, they will be resistant to anything that catalyzes it. That's human nature. And you would do the same, if the shoe were on the other foot.

With business colleagues it's even worse. They're used to dealing with you in a certain way. They're used to having a certain level of control over the relationship. And they want whatever makes them more prosperous. Sure, they might prefer it if you prosper as well, but that's not their top priority.

If your idea is so good that it changes your dynamic enough to where you need them less or, God forbid, *the market* needs them less, then they're going to resist your idea every chance they can.

Again, that's human nature.

GOOD IDEAS ALTER THE POWER BALANCE IN RELATION-SHIPS. THAT IS WHY GOOD IDEAS ARE ALWAYS INITIALLY RESISTED.

Good ideas come with a heavy burden, which is why so few people execute them. So few people can handle it.

GREAT IDEAS ALTER THE POWER BALANCE IN RELATIONSHIPS. THAT'S WHY GREAT IDEAS ARE INITIALLY RESISTED.

—yes, but...

@hugh

They were a glamorous looking crowd. Then they opened their fucking mouths

2. The idea doesn't have to be big. It just has to be yours.

The sovereignty you have over your work will inspire far more people than the actual content ever will.

WE ALL SPEND A LOT OF TIME BEING IMPRESSED by folks we've never met. Somebody featured in the media who's got a big company, a big product, a big movie, a big bestseller. Whatever.

And we spend even more time trying unsuccessfully to keep up with them. Trying to start up our own companies, our own products, our own film projects, books, and whatnot.

I'm as guilty as anyone. I tried lots of different things over the years, trying desperately to pry my career out of the jaws of mediocrity. Some to do with business, some to do with art, etc.

One evening, after one false start too many, I just gave up. Sitting at a bar, feeling a bit burned out by work and by life in general, I just started drawing on the backs of business cards for no reason. I didn't really need a reason. I just did it because it was there, because it amused me in a kind of random, arbitrary way.

Of course it was stupid. Of course it was not commercial. Of course it wasn't going to go anywhere. Of course it was a complete and utter waste of time. But in retrospect, it was this built-in futility that gave it its edge. Because it was the exact opposite of all the "Big Plans" my peers and I were used to making. It was so liberating not to have to think about all that, for a change.

It was so liberating to be doing something that didn't have to have some sort of commercial angle, for a change.

It was so liberating to be doing something that didn't have to impress anybody, for a change.

It was so liberating to be free of ambition, for a change.

It was so liberating to be doing something that wasn't a career move, for a change.

It was so liberating to have something that belonged just to me and no one else, for a change.

It was so liberating to feel complete sovereignty, for a change. To feel complete freedom, for a change. To have something that didn't require somebody else's money, or somebody else's approval, for a change.

And of course, it was then, and only then, that the outside world started paying attention.

The sovereignty you have over your work will inspire far more people than the actual content ever will. How your own sovereignty inspires other people to find their own sovereignty, their own sense of freedom and possibility, will give the work far more power than the work's objective merits ever will.

Your idea doesn't have to be big. It just has to be yours alone. The more the idea is yours alone, the more freedom you have to do something really amazing.

The more amazing, the more people will click with your idea. The more people click with your idea, the more this little thing of yours will snowball into a big thing.

That's what doodling on the backs of business cards taught me.

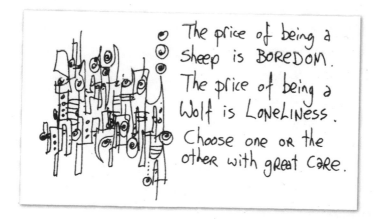

The price of being a Sheep is BOREDOM. The price of being a Wolf is LoNeLiNess. Choose one or the other with great care.

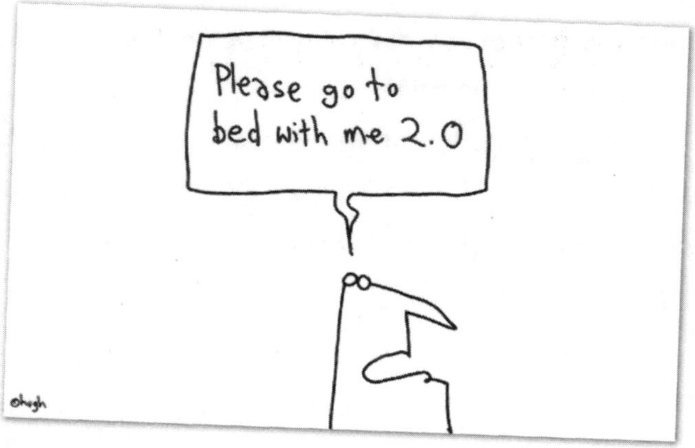
Please go to bed with me 2.0
©hugh

3. **Put the hours in.**

Doing anything worthwhile takes forever. Ninety percent of what separates successful people and failed people is time, effort, and stamina.

I GET ASKED A LOT, "YOUR BUSINESS CARD FOR- mat is very simple. Aren't you worried about somebody ripping it off?"

Standard Answer: Only if they can draw more of them than me, better than me.

What gives the work its edge is the simple fact that I've spent years drawing them. I've drawn thousands. Tens of thousands of man-hours.

So if somebody wants to rip my idea off, go ahead. If somebody wants to overtake me in the Business Card Doodle Wars, go ahead. You've got many long years in front of you. And unlike me, you won't be doing it for the joy of it. You'll be doing it for some self-loathing, ill-informed, lame-ass mercenary reason. So the years will be even longer and far, far more painful. Lucky you.

If somebody in your industry is more successful than you, it's probably because he works harder at it than you do. Sure, maybe he's more inherently talented, more adept at networking, but I don't consider that an excuse. Over time, that advantage counts for less and less. Which is why the world is full of highly talented, network-savvy, failed mediocrities.

So yeah, success means you've got a long road ahead of you, regardless. How do you best manage it?

Well, as I'm fond of saying on my blog, don't quit your day job. I didn't. I rent an office and go there every day, the same as any other regular schmoe. When I was younger and had to remind myself that there was a world outside of my head, I drew mostly while sitting at a bar in the evenings, but that got old. Even after my cartooning got successful, I still took on corporate marketing and advertising gigs, just to stay attached to the real world.

Keeping one foot in the "real world" makes everything far more manageable for me. The fact that I have another income means I don't feel pressured to do something market-friendly. Instead, I get to do whatever the hell I want. I get to do it for my own satisfaction. And I think that makes the work more powerful in the long run. It also makes it easier to carry on with it in a calm fashion, day-in-day-out, and not go crazy in insane creative bursts brought on by money worries.

The day job, which I really like, gives me something productive and interesting to do among fellow adults. It gets me out of the house in the daytime. If I were a professional cartoonist I'd just be chained to a drawing table at home all day, scribbling out a living in silence, interrupted only by frequent trips to the coffee shop. No, thank you.

Simply put, my method allows me to pace myself over the long haul, which is critical.

Stamina is utterly important. And stamina is only possible if it's managed well. People think all they need to do is endure one crazy, intense, job-free creative burst and their dreams will come true. They are wrong, they are stupidly wrong.

Being good at anything is like figure skating—the definition of being good at it is being able to make it look easy. But it never is easy. Ever. That's what the stupidly wrong people conveniently forget.

If I were just starting out writing, say, a novel or a screenplay, or maybe starting up a new software company or an online retail business, I wouldn't try to quit my job in order to make this big, dramatic, heroic-quest thing about it.

I would do something far simpler: I would find that extra hour or two in the day that belongs to nobody else but me, and I would make it productive. Put the hours in, do it for long enough, and magical, life-transforming things happen eventually. Sure, that means less time watching TV, Internet surfing, going out to dinner, or whatever.

But who cares?

Living a complete Lie
wouldn't have been so bad
if I could've just gotten
more people to
believe it...

What a happy
coincidence.
God hates the
same people
I do.

4. **Good ideas have lonely childhoods.**

This is the price you pay, every time.
There is no way of avoiding it.

THIS CHAPTER IS AS MUCH ABOUT BUSINESS as it is about "creativity." Then again, the two are rarely separate.

When I say, "Ignore Everybody," I don't mean, *Ignore all people, at all times, forever.* No, other people's feedback plays a very important role. Of course it does. It's more like, the better the idea, the more "out there" it initially will seem to other people, even people you like and respect. So there'll be a time in the beginning when you have to press on, alone, without one tenth the support you probably need. This is normal. This is to be expected. Ten years after I started doing them, drawing my "cartoons on the back of business cards" seems like a no-brainer, in terms of what it has brought me, both emotionally and to my career. But I can also clearly remember when I first started drawing them, the default reaction when I started to show my work on the back of business cards was a lot of head scratching. Sure, a few people thought they were kinda interesting and whatnot, but even to my closest friends, they seemed a complete, non-commercial exercise in futility for the New York world I was currently living in. Happily, time proved otherwise.

And again, from our first lesson, let's not forget: GOOD IDEAS ALTER THE POWER BALANCE IN RELATIONSHIPS. THAT IS WHY GOOD IDEAS ARE ALWAYS INITIALLY RESISTED. The good news is, creating an idea or brand that fights the Powers That Be can be a lot of fun, and very rewarding. The bad news is, they're called the Powers That Be for a reason—they're the ones calling the shots, they have the power. Which is why the problem of selling a new idea to the general public can sometimes be a piece of cake, compared to selling a new idea internally to your team. This is to be expected: having your boss or biggest client not like your idea and fire you hits one at a much more immediate and primal level than having some abstract housewife in rural Kansas hypothetically not liking your idea after randomly seeing it advertised somewhere. Which is why most team members in any industry are far more concerned with the power relationships inside their immediate professional circle than with what may actually be interesting and useful for the customer.

And of course, once your idea starts outgrowing its "lonely childhood," you might have a new problem to contend with. I refer to it as the *"I want to be part of something! Oh, wait, no I don't"* syndrome.

I've seen this before so many times, both firsthand and with other people. Your idea finally seems to be working, seems to be getting all sorts of traction, and all of a sudden you've got all these swarms of people trying to join the team, trying to get a piece of the action.

And then as soon as they get a foothold inside the inner circle, you soon realize they never really understood your idea in the first place, they just want to be on the winning team. And the weirdest part is, they don't seem to mind sabotaging your original idea that got them interested in the first place, in order to maintain their newfound social status. It's probably the most bizarre bit of human behavior I've ever witnessed firsthand in business, and it's *amazingly* common.

Again, this is to be expected. Good ideas don't exist in a vacuum. Good ideas exist in a social context. And not everybody has the same agenda as you.

Good ideas can have lonely young adulthoods, too.

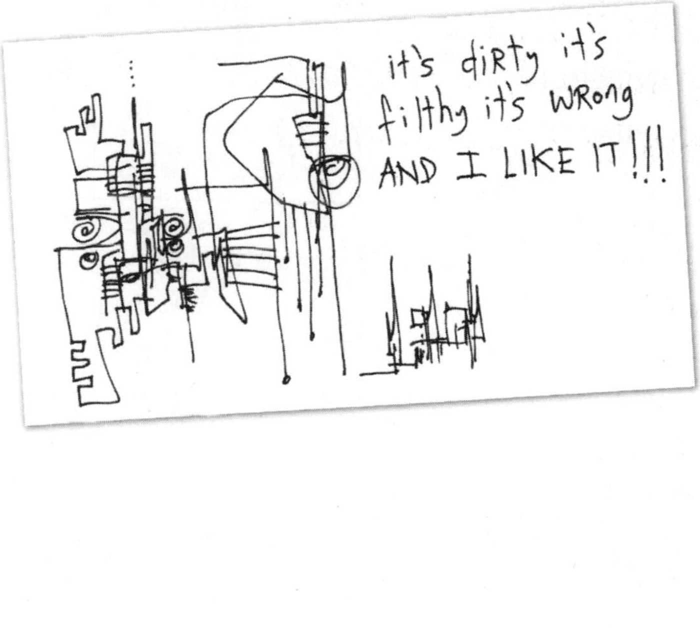
it's dirty it's
filthy it's WRong
AND I LIKE IT!!!

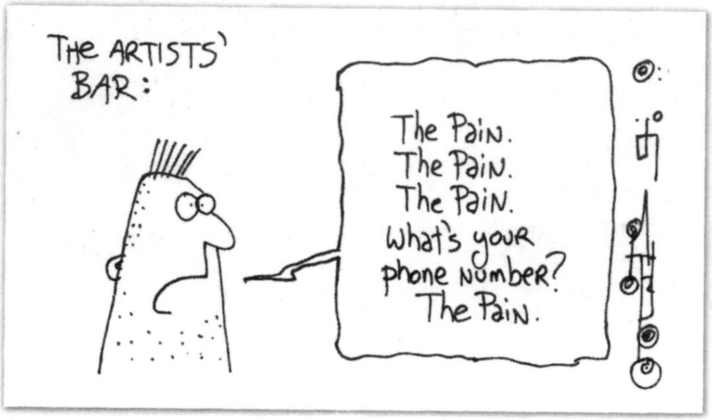
THE ARTISTS' BAR:
The Pain. The Pain. The Pain. What's your phone number? The Pain.

5. If your business plan depends on suddenly being "discovered" by some big shot, your plan will probably fail.

Nobody suddenly discovers anything. Things are made slowly and in pain.

I WAS OFFERED A QUITE SUBSTANTIAL PUBLISHing deal a few years ago. Turned it down. The company sent me a contract. I looked it over. Hmmmm . . .

Called the company back. Asked for some clarifications on some points in the contract. Never heard back from them. The deal died.

This was a very respected company. You may have even heard of it.

They just assumed I must be like all the other people they represent—hungry and desperate and willing to sign anything.

They wanted to own me, regardless of how good or bad a job they might do of helping me make my dream a reality.

That's the thing about some big publishers. They want 110 percent from you, but they don't offer to do likewise in return. To them, the artist is just one more noodle in a big bowl of pasta.

Their business model is basically to throw all the pasta against the wall, and see which noodle sticks. The ones that fall to the floor are just forgotten.

Publishers are just middlemen. That's all. If artists could remember that more often, they'd save themselves a lot of aggravation.

Not that good publishers don't exist. The groovy cats publishing this book, for example, are lovely people. But by the time we found each other, I didn't need them. I was already busy writing my blog, drawing, and doing other stuff. I already had a sizable audience, a creative outlet, and a good income stream. Though it is nice to see my name in print, it wasn't something I was dreaming about. I didn't see it as a ticket to something.

Thanks to the Internet, you can now build your own thing without having somebody else "discovering" you first. Which means when the big boys come along offering you deals, you'll be in a much better position to get *exactly* what you want from the equation. Big offers are a good thing, but personal sovereignty matters a whole lot more over the long run.

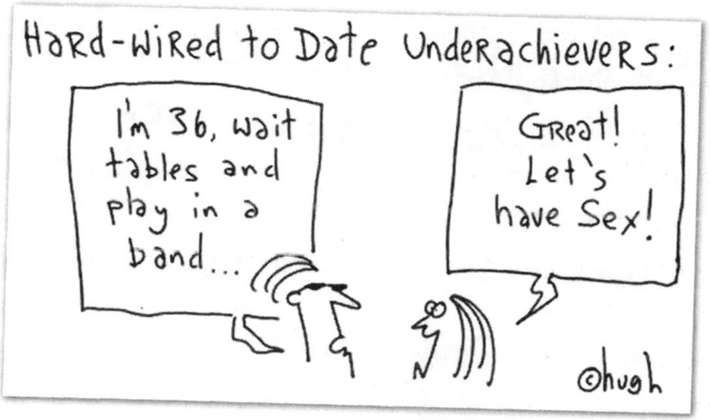
Hard-Wired to Date Underachievers:
I'm 36, wait tables and play in a band...
Great! Let's have Sex!
©hugh

Too bad the characters in the movie "Sideways" are only Fictional, because if they were Real we could find them and kill them Yay!

©hugh

6. **You are responsible for your own experience.**

Nobody can tell you if what you're doing is good, meaningful, or worthwhile. The more compelling the path, the more lonely it is.

EVERY CREATIVE PERSON IS LOOKING FOR "THE Big Idea." You know, the one that is going to catapult him or her out of the murky depths of obscurity and onto the highest planes of cultural rock stardom.

The one that's all love-at-first-sight with the Zeitgeist.

The one that's going to get them invited to all the right parties, metaphorical or otherwise.

So naturally you ask yourself, if and when you finally come up with The Big Idea, after years of toil, struggle, and doubt, how do you know whether or not it is "The One"?

Answer: You don't.

There's no glorious swelling of existential triumph.

That's not what happens.

All you get is this rather quiet, kvetchy voice inside you that seems to say, "This is totally stupid. This is utterly moronic. This is a complete waste of time. I'm going to do it anyway."

And you go do it anyway.

Second-rate ideas like glorious swellings far more. Second-rate ideas like it when the creator starts believing his own heroic-myth crap. "Me! The Artist! Me! The Bringer of Light! Me! The Creator! Me! The Undiscovered Genius!!!" It keeps the second-rate idea alive longer.

Artists don't have to suffer. Clueless No-Talent Dumb-Fucks who call themselves Artists have to suffer.

Anybody I date has to be tall, blonde, blue eyed, muscular, sporty, conservative, educated, cultured, successful, sweet, drive a Mercedes and love all my gay friends. In Return, they get my Fabulousness !!!

7. Everyone is born creative; everyone is given a box of crayons in kindergarten.

Then when you hit puberty they take the crayons away and replace them with dry, uninspiring books on algebra, history, etc. Being suddenly hit years later with the "creative bug" is just a wee voice telling you, "I'd like my crayons back, please."

SO YOU'VE GOT THE ITCH TO DO SOMETHING. Write a screenplay, start a painting, write a book, turn your recipe for fudge brownies into a proper business, build a better mousetrap, whatever. You don't know where the itch came from, it's almost like it just arrived on your doorstep, uninvited. Until now you were quite happy holding down a real job, being a regular person . . .

Until now.

You don't know if you're any good or not, but you think you could be. And the idea terrifies you. The problem is, even if you are good, you know nothing about this kind of business. You don't know any publishers or agents or venture capitalists or any of these fancy-shmancy kind of folk. You have a friend who's got a cousin in California who's into this kind of stuff, but you haven't talked to your friend for over two years . . .

Besides, if you write a book, what if you can't find a publisher? If you invent a new piece of world-changing software, what if you can't find a financial backer? If you write a screenplay, what if you can't find a producer? And what If the producer turns out to be a crook? You've always worked hard your whole life, you'll be damned if you'll put all that effort into something if there ain't no pot of gold at the end of this dumb-ass rainbow . . .

Heh. That's not your wee voice asking for the crayons back. That's your other voice, your adult voice, your boring and tedious voice trying to find a way to get the wee crayon voice to shut the hell up.

Your wee voice doesn't want you to sell something. Your wee voice wants you to make something. There's a big difference. Your wee voice doesn't give a damn about publishers, venture capitalists, or Hollywood producers.

Go ahead and make something. Make something really

special. Make something amazing that will really blow the mind of anybody who sees it.

If you try to make something just to fit your uninformed view of some hypothetical market, you will fail. If you make something special and powerful and honest and true, you will succeed.

The wee voice didn't show up because it decided you need more money, or you need to hang out with movie stars. Your wee voice came back because your soul somehow depends on it. There's something you haven't said, something you haven't done, some light that needs to be switched on, and it needs to be taken care of. Now.

So you have to listen to the wee voice or it will die . . . taking a big chunk of you along with it.

They're only crayons. You didn't fear them in kindergarten, why fear them now?

x: his lies.
y: her drinking.
z: our amusement.

8. **Keep your day job.**

I'm not just saying that for the usual reason—that is, because I think your idea will fail. I'm saying it because to suddenly quit one's job in a big ol' creative drama-queen moment is always, always, always in direct conflict with what I call "The Sex & Cash Theory."

THE SEX & CASH THEORY

The creative person basically has two kinds of jobs: One is the sexy, creative kind. Second is the kind that pays the bills. Sometimes the task at hand covers both bases, but not often. This tense duality will always play center stage. It will never be transcended.

A good example is Phil, a New York photographer friend of mine. He does really wild stuff for the small, hipster magazines—

it pays virtually nothing, but it allows him to build his portfolio. Then he'll leverage that to go off and shoot some retail catalogues for a while. Nothing too exciting, but it pays the bills.

Another example is somebody like Martin Amis, the bestselling British author. He writes "serious" novels, but also supplements his income by writing the occasional newspaper article for the London papers, or making the occasional television appearance (novel royalties are generally pathetic—even rock stars like Amis aren't immune).

Or actors. One year John Travolta will be in an ultrahip flick like *Pulp Fiction* ("Sex"), another he'll be in some forgettable, big-budget thriller like *Broken Arrow* ("Cash").

Or painters. You spend one month painting blue pictures because that's the color the celebrity collectors are buying this season ("Cash"), you spend the next month painting red pictures because secretly you despise the color blue and love the color red ("Sex").

Or geeks. You spend your weekdays writing code for a faceless corporation ("Cash"), then you spend your evenings and weekends writing anarchic, weird computer games to amuse your techie friends ("Sex").

It's balancing the need to make a good living while still maintaining one's creative sovereignty. My MO is drawing cartoons and writing in my blog ("Sex"), coupled with my day job. (See tip # 3 for more details on the latter.)

I'm thinking about the young writer who has to wait tables to pay the bills, in spite of her writing appearing in all the cool and hip magazines . . . who dreams of one day not having her life divided so harshly.

Well, over time the "harshly" bit might go away, but not the "divided."

This tense duality will always play center stage. It will never be transcended.

And nobody is immune. Not the struggling waiter, nor the movie star.

As soon as you accept this, I mean really accept this, for some reason your career starts moving ahead faster. I don't know why this happens. It's the people who refuse to cleave their lives this way—who just want to start Day One by quitting their current crappy day job and moving straight on over to bestselling author—well, they never make it.

Anyway, it's called "The Sex & Cash Theory." Keep it under your pillow.

Anywhere that has a
lot of cute, smart,
young, successful, sexy
women who want to
fuck is going to be
expensive.

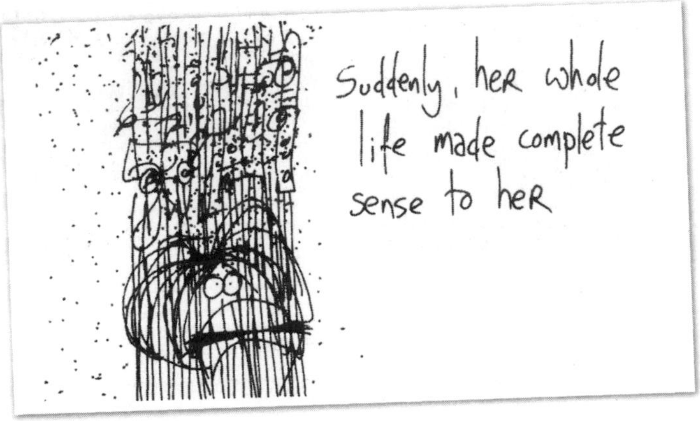
Suddenly, her whole life made complete sense to her

9. **Companies that squelch creativity can no longer compete with companies that champion creativity.**

Nor can you bully a subordinate into becoming a genius.

SINCE THE MODERN, SCIENTIFICALLY CONCEIVED corporation was invented in the early half of the twentieth century, creativity has been sacrificed in favor of forwarding the interests of the "team player."

Fair enough. There was more money in doing it that way; that's why they did it.

There's only one problem. Team players are not very good at

creating value on their own. They are not autonomous; they need a team in order to exist.

So now corporations are awash with nonautonomous thinkers.

"I don't know. What do you think?"
"I don't know. What do you think?"
"I don't know. What do you think?"
"I don't know. What do you think?"
"I don't know. What do you think?"
"I don't know. What do you think?"

And so on.

Creating an economically viable entity where lack of original thought is handsomely rewarded creates a rich, fertile environment for parasites to breed. And that's exactly what's been happening. So now we have millions upon millions of human tapeworms thriving in the Western world, making love to their PowerPoint presentations, feasting on the creativity of others.

What happens to an ecology when the parasite level reaches critical mass?

The ecology dies.

If you're creative, if you can think independently, if you can articulate passion, if you can override the fear of being wrong, then your company needs you now more than it ever did. And now your company can no longer afford to pretend that isn't the case.

So dust off your horn and start tooting it. Exactly.

And if you don't see yourself as particularly creative, that's not reality, that's a self-imposed limitation. Only you can decide whether you want to carry that around with you forever. Life is short.

You are the most important person in my Life. Please stop laughing at me.

10. Everybody has their own private Mount Everest they were put on this earth to climb.

You may never reach the summit; for that you will be forgiven. But if you don't make at least one serious attempt to get above the snow line, years later you will find yourself lying on your deathbed, and all you will feel is emptiness.

THIS METAPHORICAL MOUNT EVEREST DOESN'T have to manifest itself as "Art." For some people, yes, it might be a novel or a painting. But Art is just one path up the mountain, one of many. With others the path may be something more down-to-earth. Making a million dollars, raising a family, owning the most Burger King franchises in the tristate area, building some crazy oversized model airplane, starting an Internet company, opening up a small fashion boutique, opening a bar, the list has no end.

Whatever. Let's talk about you now. Your mountain. Your private Mount Everest. Yes, that one. Exactly.

Let's say you never climb it. Do you have a problem with that? Can you just say to yourself, "Never mind, I never really wanted it anyway," and take up stamp collecting instead?

Well, you could try. But I wouldn't believe you. I think it's not OK for you never to try to climb it. And I think you agree with me. Otherwise you wouldn't have read this far.

So it looks like you're going to have to climb the frickin' mountain. Deal with it.

My advice? You don't need my advice. You really don't. The biggest piece of advice I could give anyone would be this: "Admit that your own private Mount Everest exists. That is half the battle."

And you've already done that. You really have. Otherwise, again, you wouldn't have read this far.

Rock on.

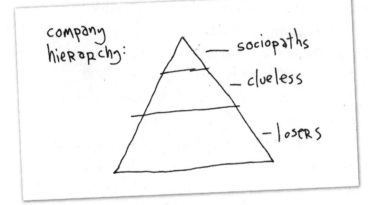

company hierarchy:

— sociopaths

— clueless

— losers

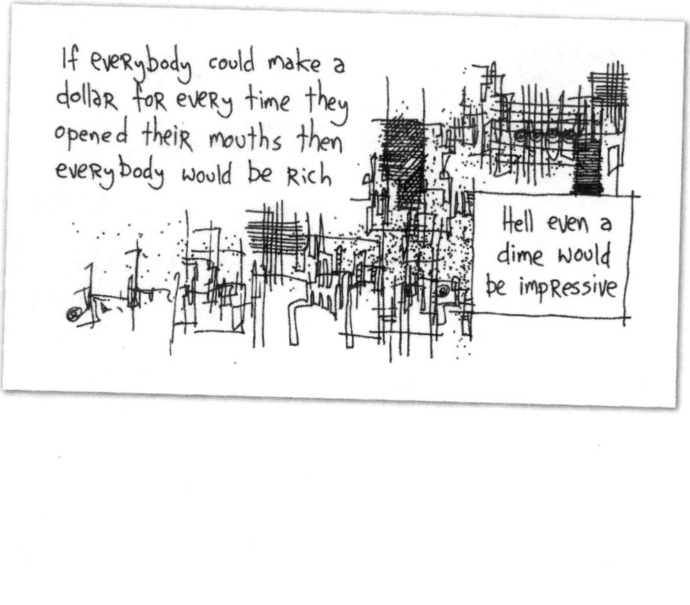
If everybody could make a dollar for every time they opened their mouths then everybody would be rich
Hell even a dime would be impressive

11. The more talented somebody is, the less they need the props.

Meeting a person who wrote a masterpiece on the back of a deli menu would not surprise me. Meeting a person who wrote a masterpiece with a silver Cartier fountain pen on an antique writing table in an airy SoHo loft would *seriously* surprise me.

ABRAHAM LINCOLN WROTE THE GETTYSBURG Address on a piece of ordinary stationery that he had borrowed from the friend whose house he was staying at.

Ernest Hemingway wrote with a simple fountain pen. Somebody else did the typing, but only much later.

Van Gogh rarely painted with more than six colors on his palette.

I draw on the back of small business cards. Whatever.

There's no correlation between creativity and equipment ownership. None. Zilch. Nada.

Actually, as the artist gets more into her thing, and as she gets more successful, the number of tools tends to go down. She knows what works for her. Expending mental energy on stuff wastes time. She's a woman on a mission. She's got a deadline. She's got some rich client breathing down her neck. The last thing she wants is to spend three weeks learning how to use a router drill if she doesn't need to.

A fancy tool just gives the second-rater one more pillar to hide behind.

Which is why there are so many second-rate art directors with state-of-the-art Macintosh computers.

Which is why there are so many hack writers with state-of-the-art laptops.

Which is why there are so many crappy photographers with state-of-the-art digital cameras.

Which is why there are so many unremarkable painters with expensive studios in trendy neighborhoods.

Hiding behind pillars, all of them.

Pillars do not help; they hinder. The more mighty the pillar, the more you end up relying on it psychologically, the more it gets in your way.

And this applies to business as well.

Which is why there are so many failing businesses with fancy offices.

Which is why there's so many failing businessmen spending a fortune on fancy suits and expensive yacht club memberships.

Again, hiding behind pillars.

Successful people, artists and nonartists alike, are very good at spotting pillars. They're very good at doing without them. Even more important, once they've spotted a pillar, they're very good at quickly getting rid of it.

Good pillar management is one of the most valuable talents you can have on the planet. If you have it, I envy you. If you don't, I pity you.

Sure, nobody's perfect. We all have our pillars. We seem to need them. You are never going to live a pillar-free existence. Neither am I.

All we can do is keep asking the question, "Is this a pillar?" about every aspect of our business, our craft, our reason for being alive, and go from there. The more we ask, the better we get at spotting pillars, the more quickly the pillars vanish.

Ask. Keep asking. And then ask again. Stop asking and you're dead.

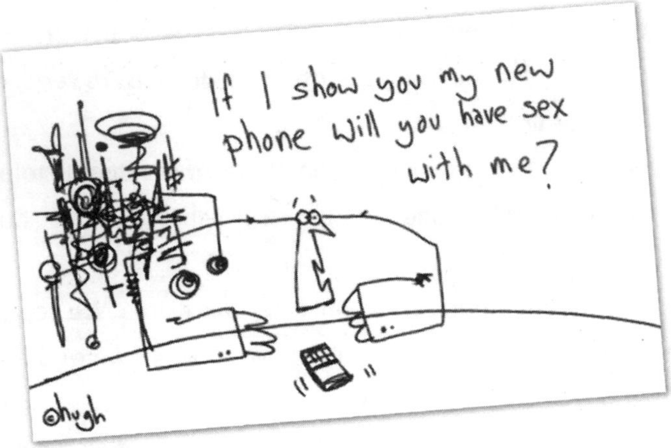
If I show you my new phone will you have sex with me?
©hugh

a loose confederation of skunk works....
joined by insanity

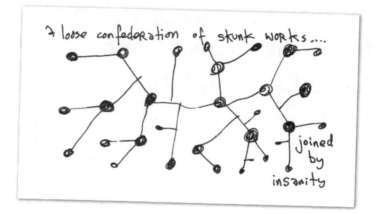

12. **Don't try to stand out from the crowd; avoid crowds altogether.**

Your plan for getting your work out there has to be as original as the actual work, perhaps even more so. The work has to create a totally new market. There's no point trying to do the same thing as 250,000 other young hopefuls, waiting for a miracle. All existing business models are wrong. Find a new one.

WE'VE SEEN IT SO MANY TIMES. CALL HIM TED. A young kid in the big city, just off the bus, wanting to be a famous something: artist, writer, musician, film director, entrepreneur, software genius, whatever. He's full of fire, passion, and ideas. And then you meet Ted again five or ten years later, and he's still tending bar at the same restaurant. He's not a kid anymore. But he's still no closer to his dream.

His voice is still as defiant as ever, certainly, but there's an emptiness to his words that wasn't there before.

Yeah, well, Ted probably chose a very well-trodden path. Write novel, be discovered, publish bestseller, sell movie rights, retire rich in five years. Or whatever.

No worries that there's probably three million other novelists/actors/musicians/painters/dreamers with the same plan. But of course, Ted's special. Of course his fortune will defy the odds eventually. Of course. That's what he keeps telling you, as he refills your glass.

Is your plan of a similar ilk? If it is, then I'd be concerned.

When I started the business card cartoons I was lucky; at the time I had a pretty well-paid corporate job in New York that I liked. The idea of quitting it in order to join the ranks of Bohemia didn't even occur to me. What, leave Manhattan for Brooklyn? Ha. Not bloody likely. I was just doing it to amuse myself in the evenings, to give me something to do at the bar while I waited for my date to show up or whatever.

There was no commercial incentive or larger agenda governing my actions. If I wanted to draw on the back of a business card instead of a "proper" medium, I could. If I wanted to use a four-letter word, I could. If I wanted to ditch the standard figurative format and draw psychotic abstractions instead, I could. There was no flashy media or publishing executive to keep happy. And even better, there was no artist-lifestyle archetype to conform to.

It gave me a lot of freedom. That freedom paid off in spades later.

Question how much freedom your path affords you. Be utterly ruthless about it.

It's your freedom that will get you to where you want to go. Blind faith in an oversubscribed, vainglorious myth will only hinder you.

Is your plan unique? Is there nobody else doing it? Then I'd be excited. A little scared, maybe, but excited.

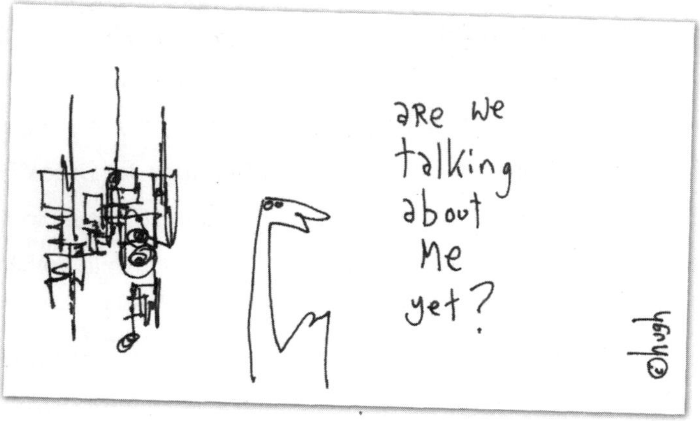
are we talking about me yet?
©hugh

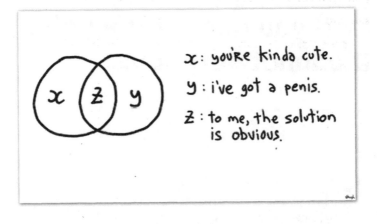

x: you're kinda cute.

y: i've got a penis.

z: to me, the solution is obvious.

13. **If you accept the pain, it cannot hurt you.**

The pain of making the necessary sacrifices always hurts more than you think it's going to. I know. It sucks. That being said, doing something seriously creative is one of the most amazing experiences one can have, in this or any other lifetime. If you can pull it off, it's worth it. Even if you don't end up pulling it off, you'll learn many incredible, magical, valuable things. It's not doing it—when you know full well you had the opportunity—that hurts far more than any failure.

FRANKLY, I THINK YOU'RE BETTER OFF DOING something on the assumption that you will *not* be rewarded for it, that it will *not* receive the recognition it deserves, that it will *not* be worth the time and effort invested in it.

The obvious advantage to this angle is, of course, if anything good comes of it, then it's an added bonus.

The second, more subtle and profound advantage is that by scuppering all hope of worldly and social betterment from the creative act, you are finally left with only one question to answer:

Do you make this damn thing exist or not?

And once you can answer that truthfully for yourself, the rest is easy.

Wake up and tell me that you love me...

hugh

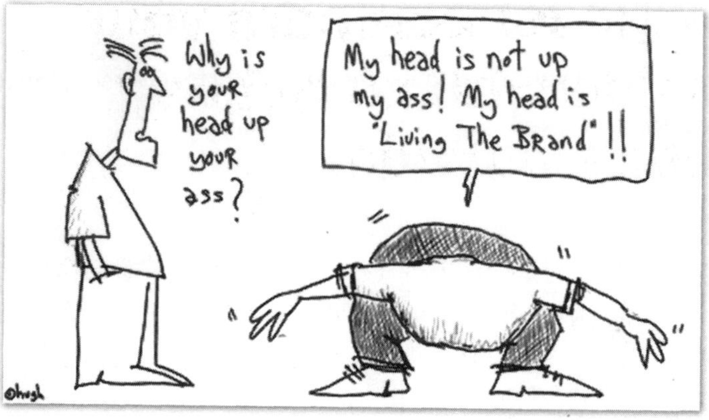
Why is your head up your ass?
My head is not up my ass! My head is "Living The Brand"!!
©hugh

14. **Never compare your inside with somebody else's outside.**

The more you practice your craft, the less you confuse worldly rewards with spiritual rewards, and vice versa. Even if your path never makes any money or furthers your career, that's still worth a *ton*.

WHEN I WAS SIXTEEN OR SEVENTEEN IN EDIN-burgh I vaguely knew this guy who owned a shop called Cinders, on St. Stephen's Street. It specialized in restoring antique fireplaces. Cinders's modus operandi was very simple. Buy original Georgian and Victorian chimneypieces from old, dilapidated houses for ten cents on the dollar, give them a loving but expedient makeover in the workshop, sell them at vast profit to yuppies.

Back then I was insatiably curious about how people made a living (I still am). So one day, while sitting on his stoop, I chatted with the Fireplace Guy about it.

He told me about the finer points of his trade—the hunting through old houses, the craftsmanship, the customer relations, and of course the profit.

The fellow seemed quite proud of his job. From how he described it he seemed to like his trade and to be making a decent living. Scotland was going through a bit of a recession at the time; unemployment was high, money was tight; I guess for an aging hippie things could've been a lot worse.

Very few kids ever said, "Gosh, when I grow up I'm going to be a Fireplace Guy!" It's not the most obvious trade in the world. I asked him about how he fell into it.

"I used to be an antiques dealer," he said. "People who spend a lot of money on antiques also seem to spend a lot of money restoring their houses. So I sort of got the whiff of opportunity just by talking to people in my antiques shop. Also, there are too many antique dealers in Edinburgh crowding the market, so I was looking for an easier way to make a living."

Like the best jobs in the world, it just kinda sorta happened.

"Well, some of the fireplaces are real beauties," I said. "It must be hard parting with them."

"No, it isn't," he said (and this is the part I remember most). "I mean, I like them, but because they take up so much room—they're so big and bulky—I'm relieved to be rid of them once they're sold. I just want them out of the shop ASAP and the cash in my pocket. Selling them is easy for me. Unlike antiques. I always loved antiques, so I was always falling in love with the inventory, I always wanted to hang on to my best stuff. I'd always subconsciously price them too high in order to keep them from leaving the shop."

Being young and idealistic, I told him I thought that was quite sad. Why choose to sell a "mere product" (e.g. chimneypieces) when instead you could make your living selling something you really care about (e.g. antiques)? Surely the latter would be a preferable way to work?

"The first rule of business," he said, chuckling at my naïveté, "is never sell something you love. Otherwise, you may as well be selling your children."

Fifteen years later I'm at a bar in New York. Some friend-of-a-friend is looking at my cartoons. He asks me if I publish. I tell him I don't. Tell him it's just a hobby. Tell him about my advertising job.

"Man, why the hell are you in advertising?" he says, pointing to my portfolio. "You should be doing this. Galleries and stuff. T-shirts!"

"Advertising's just chimneypieces," I say, speaking into my glass.

"What the hell?"

"Never mind."

Film student and
ART student
duking it out....
No, I'M more annoying!
No, I'M more annoying!

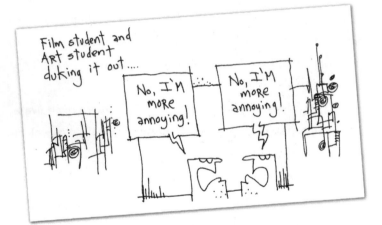

I'm not a
Loser.
I just
happen to like
pleading for sex.

15. **Dying young is overrated.**

I've seen so many young people take the "Gotta do the drugs and booze thing to make me a better artist" route over the years. A choice that wasn't smart, original, effective, healthy, or ended happily.

IT'S A FAMILIAR STORY: A KID READS ABOUT Charlie Parker or Jimi Hendrix or Charles Bukowski and somehow decides that their poetic but flawed example somehow gives him permission and/or absolution to spend the next decade or two drowning in his own metaphorical vomit.

Of course, the older you get, the more casualties of this foolishness you meet. The more time they have had to ravage their lives. The more pathetic they seem. And the less remarkable work they seem to have to show for it, for all their "amazing experiences" and "special insights."

The smarter and more talented the artist is, the less likely he will choose this route. Sure, he might screw around a wee bit while he's young and stupid, but he will move on quicker than most.

But the kid thinks it's all about talent; he thinks it's all about "potential." He underestimates how much time, discipline, and stamina also play their part. Sure, like Bukowski et al., there are exceptions. But that is why we like their stories when we're young. Because they are exceptional stories. And every kid with a guitar or a pen or a paintbrush or an idea for a new business wants to be exceptional. Every kid underestimates his competition, and overestimates his chances. Every kid is a sucker for the idea that there's a way to make it without having to do the actual hard work.

So the bars of West Hollywood, London, and New York are awash with people throwing their lives away in the desperate hope of finding a shortcut, any shortcut. And a lot of them aren't even young anymore, their B-plans having been washed away by beer and vodka years ago.

Meanwhile the competition is at home, working their asses off.

The dream had vanished.
Unfortunately the
Lifestyle Remained.

My wine ...
my passion ...
my cool sunglasses ...

@hugh

16. **The most important thing a creative person can learn professionally is where to draw the red line that separates what you are willing to do from what you are not.**

Art suffers the moment other people start paying for it. The more you need the money, the more people will tell you what to do. The less control you will have. The more bullshit you will have to swallow. The less joy it will bring. Know this and plan accordingly.

NOT LONG AGO I HEARD CHRIS WARE, CURRENTLY
one of the top two or three most critically acclaimed cartoonists
on the planet, describe his profession as "unrewarding."

When the guy at the top of the ladder you're climbing describes
the view from the top as "unrewarding," be concerned. Heh.

I knew Chris back in college, at the University of Texas. Later,
in the early 1990s, I knew him from hanging around Wicker Park
in Chicago, that famous arty neighborhood, while he was getting
his master's from the School of the Art Institute of Chicago, and
I was working as a junior copywriter in a downtown ad agency.
We weren't that close, but we had mutual friends. He's a nice
guy. Smart as hell.

So I've watched him over the years go from talented under-
graduate to famous rock star comic strip guy. Nice to see,
certainly—it's encouraging when people you know get deserv-
edly famous. But also by watching him, I got to see firsthand the
realities of being a professional cartoonist, both good and bad.
It's helpful to get a snapshot of actual reality.

His example really clarified a lot for me about ten to fifteen years ago, when I got to the point where my cartoons were good enough that I could actually consider doing it professionally. I looked at the market, saw the kind of life Chris and others like him had, saw the people in the business calling the shots, saw the kind of deluded planet most cartoon publishers were living on, and went, "Naaaah."

Thinking about it some more, I think one of the main reasons I stayed in advertising for so many years is simply because hearing "Change that ad" ticks me off a lot less than "Change that cartoon." Though the compromises one has to make writing ads can often be tremendous, there's only so much you have to take personally. It's their product, it's their money, so it's easier to maintain healthy boundaries. With pure cartooning, I invariably found this impossible.

The most important thing a creative person can learn professionally is where to draw the red line that separates what you are willing to do from what you are not. It is this red line that demarcates your sovereignty; that defines your own private creative domain. What crap you are willing to take, and what crap you're not. What you are willing to relinquish control over, and what you aren't. What price you are willing to pay, and what price you aren't. Everybody is different; everybody has their own red line. Everybody has their own Sex & Cash Theory.

When I see somebody "suffering for their art," it's usually a case of their not knowing where that red line is, not knowing where the sovereignty lies.

Somehow he thought that sleazy producer wouldn't make him butcher his film with pointless rewrites, but Alas! Somehow he thought that gallery owner would turn out to be a competent businessman, but Alas! Somehow he thought that publisher would promote his new novel properly, but Alas! Somehow he thought that venture capitalist would be less of an asshole about the start-up's cash flow, but Alas! Somehow he thought that CEO would support his new marketing initiative, but Alas!

Knowing where to draw the red line is like knowing yourself or knowing who your real friends are. Some people find it easier to do than others. Life is unfair.

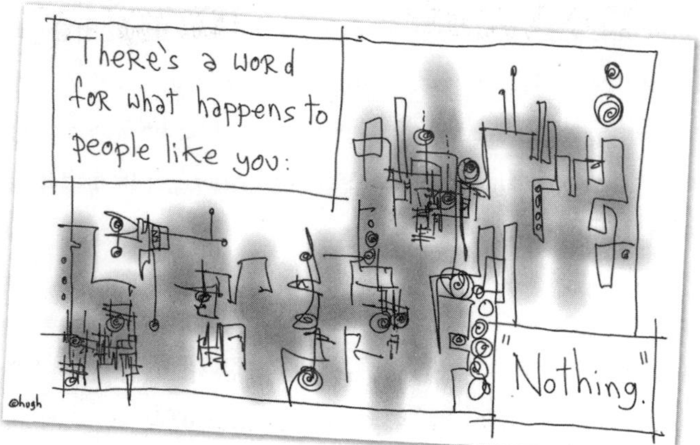
There's a word for what happens to people like you:
"Nothing."
@hugh

17. **The world is changing.**

Some people are hip to it, others are not. If you want to be able to afford groceries in five years, I'd recommend listening closely to the former and avoiding the latter. Just my two cents.

YOUR JOB IS PROBABLY WORTH 50 PERCENT of what it was in real terms ten years ago. And who knows? It may very well not exist in five to ten years.

We all saw the traditional biz model in my former industry, advertising, start going down the tubes ten years or so ago. Our first reaction was "work harder."

It didn't work. People got shafted by the thousands. It's a cold world out there.

We thought being talented would save our asses. We thought working late and on weekends would save our asses. Nope.

We thought the Internet and all that Next Big Thing, new media and new technology stuff would save our asses. We thought it would fill the holes in the ever more intellectually bankrupt solutions we were offering our clients. Nope.

Whatever. Regardless of how the world changes, regardless of what new technologies, business models, and social architectures are coming down the pike, the one thing "The New Realities" cannot take away from you is trust.

The people you trust and vice versa are what will feed you and pay for your kids' college. Nothing else.

This is true if you're an artist, writer, doctor, techie, lawyer, banker, or bartender.

In other words: Stop worrying about technology. Start worrying about people who trust you.

In order to navigate the New Realities you have to be creative—not just within your particular profession, but in *everything*. Your way of looking at the world will need to become ever more fertile and original. And this isn't just true for artists, writers, techies, creative directors, and CEOs; this is true for *everybody*. Janitors, receptionists, and bus drivers, too. The game has just been ratcheted up a notch.

The old ways are dead. And you need people around you who concur.

That means hanging out more with the creative people, the freaks, the real visionaries, than you're already doing. Thinking more about what their needs are, and responding accordingly.

It doesn't matter what industry we're talking about—architecture, advertising, petrochemicals—they're around, they're easy enough to find if you make the effort, if you've got something worthwhile to offer in return. Avoid the dullards; avoid the folk who play it safe. They can't help you anymore. Their stability model no longer offers that much stability. They are extinct; they are extinction.

Never try to sell a meteor to a Dinosaur. It wastes your time and annoys the Dinosaur.

©hugh

I'd love to go home with you tonight but frankly I came here to talk about me.

18. Merit can be bought. Passion can't.

The only people who can change the world are people who want to. And not everybody does.

HUMAN BEINGS HAVE THIS THING I CALL THE "Pissed Off Gene." It's that bit of our psyche that makes us utterly dissatisfied with our lot, no matter how kindly Fortune smiles upon us.

It's there for a reason. Back in our early caveman days, being pissed off made us more likely to get off our butts, get out of the cave and into the tundra hunting woolly mammoth, so we'd have something to eat for supper. It's a survival mechanism. Damn useful then, damn useful now.

It's this same Pissed Off Gene that makes us want to create

anything in the first place—drawings, violin sonatas, meat packing companies, Web sites. This same gene drove us to discover how to make a fire, the wheel, the bow and arrow, indoor plumbing, the personal computer, the list is endless.

Part of understanding the creative urge is understanding that it's primal. Wanting to change the world is not a noble calling, it's a primal calling.

We think we're "Providing a superior integrated logistic system" or "Helping America to really taste Freshness." In fact we're just pissed off and want to get the hell out of the cave and kill the woolly mammoth.

Your business either lets you go hunt the woolly mammoth or it doesn't. Of course, as with so many white-collar jobs these days, you might very well be offered a ton of money to sit in the corner-office cave and pretend that you're hunting, even if you're not, even if you're just pushing pencils. That is sad. What's even sadder is that you agreed to take the money.

the market for
something to believe in

is infinite

conversation: a
useful device mostly
used to find out
how much somebody
is paying for
their apartment

19. **Avoid the Watercooler Gang.**

They're a well-meaning bunch, but they get in the way eventually.

BACK WHEN I WORKED FOR A LARGE ADVERTIS-
ing agency as a young rookie, it used to bother me how much
the "Watercooler Gang" just kvetched all the time. The "Watercooler Gang" was my term for what was still allowed to exist in
the industry back then. Packs of second-tier creatives, many
years past their sell-by date, being squeezed by the creative
directors for every last ounce of juice they had, till it came time
to fire them on the cheap. Taking too many trips to the watercooler and coming back drunk from lunch far too often. Working
late nights and weekends on all the boring-but-profitable
accounts. Squeeze, squeeze, squeeze.

I remember some weeks where one could easily spend half an hour a day listening to Ted complain.

Ted used to have a window office but now had a cube, ever since that one disastrous meeting with Client X. He would come visit me in my cube at least once a day and start his thing. Complain, complain, complain... about whatever: how Josh-the-Golden-Boy was a shit writer and a complete phony... or how they bought Little-Miss-Hot-Pants' ad instead of his, "Even though mine was the best in the room and every bastard there knew it."

Like I said, whatever.

It was endless... yak yak yak... Oy vey! Ted, I love ya, you're a great guy, but shut the hell up....

In retrospect it was Ted's example that taught me a very poignant lesson—back then I was still too young and naive to have learned it by that point—that your office could be awash with every ad award in existence, Clios and One Show awards (those are the big ones in the industry), yet your career could still be down the sinkhole.

Don't get me wrong—my career there was a complete disaster. This is not a case of one of the Alphas mocking the Betas. This is a Gamma mocking the Betas.

I'm having lunch with my associate John, who's about the same age as I am. We started working at the agency about the same time. We're eating cheap and cheerful Thai food, just down the road from the agency.

"I gotta get out of this company," I say.

"I thought you liked your job," says John.

"I do," I say. "But the only reason they like having me around is because I'm still young and cheap. The minute I am no longer either, I'm dead meat."

"Like Ted," says John.

"Yeah, him and the rest of the Watercooler Gang."

"The Watercoolies." John laughs.

So we had a good chuckle about our poor, hapless elders. We weren't that sympathetic, frankly. Their lives might have been hell then, but they had already had their glory moments. They had won their awards, flown off to the Bahamas to shoot toilet paper ads with famous movie stars and all that. Unlike us young'uns. John and I had only been out of college a couple of years and had yet to make our mark on the industry we had entered with about as much passion and hope as anybody alive.

We had sold a few newspaper ads now and then, some magazine spreads, but the TV stuff was still well beyond reach. So far the agency we had worked for had yet to allow us to shine. Was this our fault or theirs? Maybe a little bit of both, but back then it was all "Their fault, dammit!" Of course, everything is "Their fault, dammit" when you're twenty-four.

I quit my job about a year later. John stayed on with the agency for whatever reason, then a few years later got married, with his first kid following soon after. Suddenly with a family to support, he couldn't afford to get fired. The creative director knew this and started to squeeze.

"You don't mind working this weekend, John, do you? Good. I knew you wouldn't. We all know how much the team relies on you to deliver at crunch time—that's why we value you so highly, John, wouldn't you say?"

Last time I saw John he was working at this horrible little agency for a fraction of his former salary. Turns out the big agency had tossed him out about a week after his kid's second birthday.

We're sitting there at the Thai restaurant again, having lunch for old time's sake. We're having a good time, talking about the usual artsy-fartsy stuff we always do. It's a great conversation, marred only by the fact that when I look at John, the word "Watercooler" keeps popping into my head, uninvited.

You think magazines are disposable?

You should see the people who work for them.

...I'm going to be
in town Thursday
and Friday night...
I need sex, and
you probably need
to be taken out
somewhere decent
for once.... Call me!
(Beeeep!)

20. Sing in your own voice.

Picasso was a terrible colorist. Turner couldn't paint human beings worth a damn. Saul Steinberg's formal drafting skills were appalling. T. S. Eliot had a full-time day job. Henry Miller was a wildly uneven writer. Bob Dylan can't sing or play guitar.

BUT THAT DIDN'T STOP THEM, RIGHT?

So I guess the next question is, "Why not?"

I have no idea. Why should it? No one person can be good at everything. The really good artists, the really successful entrepreneurs, figure out how to circumvent their limitations, figure out how to turn their strengths into weaknesses. The fact that Turner couldn't draw human beings very well left him *no choice* but to improve his landscape paintings, which have no equal.

Had Bob Dylan been more of a technical virtuoso, he might not have felt the need to give his song lyrics such power and resonance.

Don't make excuses. Just shut the hell up and get on with it. Time waits for no one.

I will
love you
forever

So long as
the sex
maintains its
current level

21. The choice of media is irrelevant.

Every medium's greatest strength is also its greatest weakness. Every form of media is a set of fundamental compromises; one is not "higher" than the others. A painting doesn't do much, it just sits there on a wall. That's the best and worst thing about it. Film combines sound, movement, photography, music, acting. That's the best and worst thing about it. Prose just uses words arranged in linear form to get its point across. That's the best and worst thing about it, etc.

BACK IN COLLEGE I WAS AN ENGLISH MAJOR. I had no aspirations for teaching, writing, or academe, it was just a subject I could get consistently high grades in. Plus I liked to read books and write papers, so it worked well enough for me.

Most of my friends were Liberal Arts Majors, but there the similarity ended. We never really went to class together. Sure, we'd meet up in the evenings and weekends, but I never really socialized with people in my classes that much.

So it was always surprising to me to meet the Art Majors: fine arts, film, drama, architecture, etc. They seemed to live in each other's pockets. They all seemed to work, eat, and sleep together. Lots of bonding going on. Lots of collaboration. Lots of incest. Lots of speeches about the sanctity of their craft.

Well, a cartoon only needs one person to make it. Same with a piece of writing. No Big Group Hug required. So all this sex-fueled socialism was rather alien to me, even if parts of it seemed very appealing.

During my second year at college I started getting my cartoons published, and not just in the school paper. Suddenly I found meeting girls easy. I was very happy about that, I can assure you, but life carried on pretty much the same.

I suppose my friends thought the cartooning gigs were neat or whatever, but it wasn't really anything that affected our friendship. It was just something I did on the side, the way other people restored old cars or kept a darkroom for their camera.

My cartooning MO was and still is to just have a normal life, be a regular schmoe, with a terrific hobby on the side. It's not exactly rocket science.

This attitude seemed fairly alien to the Art Majors I met. Their chosen art form seemed more like a religion to them. It was serious. It was important. It was a big part of their identity, and it almost seemed to them that humanity's very existence totally depended on their being able to pursue their dream as a handsomely rewarded profession, etc.

Don't get me wrong, I knew some Art Majors who were absolutely brilliant. One or two of them are famous now. And I can see if you've got a special talent how the need to seriously pursue it becomes important.

But looking back, I also see a lot of screwy kids who married themselves to their "Art!" for the wrong reasons. Not because they had anything particularly unique or visionary to say, not because they had any remarkable talent, but because it was cool. Because it was sexy. Because it was hip. Because it gave them something to talk about at keg parties. Because it was easier than having to think about getting a real job after graduation.

I'm of two minds about this. One part of me thinks it's good for kids to mess around with insanely high ambitions, and maybe one or two of them will make it, maybe one or two will survive the cull. That's what being young is all about, and I think it's wonderful.

The other side of me wants to tell these kids to beware of choosing difficult art forms for the wrong reasons. You can wing it while you're young, but it's not till your youth is over that the Devil starts seeking out his due. And that's never pretty. I've seen it happen more than once to some very dear, sweet people, and it's really heartbreaking to watch.

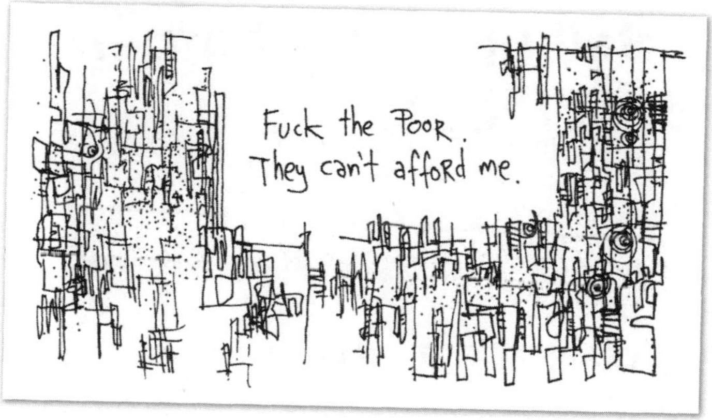
Fuck the Poor.
They can't afford me.

22. **Selling out is harder than it looks.**

Diluting your product to make it more
"commercial" will just make people like it less.

MANY YEARS AGO, BARELY OUT OF COLLEGE, I
started schlepping my portfolio around the ad agencies, looking
for my first job.

One fine day a creative director in a big corner office
downtown kindly agreed for me to come show him my work.
Hooray!

So I came to his office and showed him my work. Frankly, the
work was bloody awful. All of it. Imagine the worst, cheesiest "I
used to wash with Sudso but now I wash with Lemon-Fresh Rinso
Extreme" vapid-housewife crap. Only far worse than that.

The creative director was a nice guy. You could tell he didn't think much of my work, though he was far too polite to blurt it out. Finally he quietly confessed that it wasn't doing much for him.

"Well, the target market is middle-class housewives," I rambled. "They're quite conservative, so I thought I'd better tone it down...."

"You can tone it down once you've gotten the job and once the client comes after your ass with a red-hot poker and tells you to tone it down." He laughed. "Till then, show me the toned-up version."

This story doesn't just happen in advertising. It happens everywhere.

It's hard to sell out if nobody has bought in.

I'm not scared of commitment. I'm scared of you.

23. **Nobody cares. Do it for yourself.**

Everybody is too busy with their own lives to give a damn about your book, painting, screenplay, etc., especially if you haven't finished it yet. And the ones who aren't too busy you don't want in your life anyway.

MAKING A BIG DEAL OVER YOUR CREATIVE shtick to other people is the kiss of death. That's all I have to say on the subject.

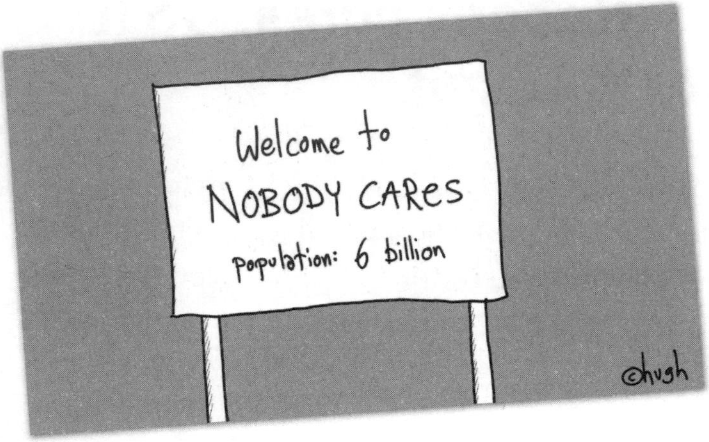
Welcome to
NOBODY CARES
population: 6 billion
©hugh

Oh No
Oh God
Oh No
The couple
sitting at
the next
table are
tacky and
gross

24. **Worrying about "Commercial vs. Artistic" is a complete waste of time.**

You can argue about "Selling Out" versus "Artistic Purity" till the cows come home. People were kvetching about it in 1850, and they'll be kvetching about it in 2150.

VIGOROUS DEBATE ABOUT COMMERCIALISM IN art is a path well trodden, and not a place where one is going to come up with many new, earth-shattering insights. But a lot of people like to dwell on it because it keeps them from ever having to journey into unknown territory. It's safe. It allows you to have strong emotions and opinions without any real risk to yourself.

Without your having to do any of the actual hard work involved in the making and selling of something you believe in.

To me, it's not about whether Tom Clancy sells truckloads of books or a Nobel Prize winner sells diddly-squat. Those are just ciphers, external distractions. To me, it's about what *you* are going to do with the short time you have left on this earth. Different criteria altogether.

Frankly, how a person nurtures and develops his or her own "creative sovereignty," with or without the help of the world at large, is in my opinion a much more interesting subject.

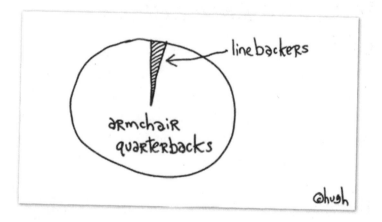

The worst thing about being a
Beta Male is that all women
secretly despise you.

@hugh

25. **Don't worry about finding inspiration. It comes eventually.**

Inspiration precedes the desire to create, not the other way around.

ONE OF THE REASONS I GOT INTO DRAWING cartoons on the back of business cards was that I could carry them around with me. Living in downtown New York, as I did back then, you spend a lot of time walking around the place. I wanted an art form that was perfect for that.

So if I was walking down the street and I suddenly got hit with the itch to draw something, I could just nip over to the nearest park bench or coffee shop, pull out a blank card from my bag and get busy doing my thing. Seamless. Effortless. No fuss. I like it.

Before, when I was doing larger works, every time I got an idea while walking down the street I'd have to quit what I was doing and schlep back to my studio while the inspiration was still buzzing around in my head. Nine times out of ten the inspired moment would have passed by the time I got back, rendering the whole exercise futile. Sure, I'd get drawing anyway, but it always seemed I was drawing a memory, not something happening at that very moment.

If you're arranging your life in such a way that you need to make a lot of fuss between feeling the itch and getting to work, you're putting the cart before the horse. You're probably creating a lot of counterproductive "Me, the Artist, I must create, I must leave something to posterity" melodrama. Not interesting for you or for anyone else.

You have to find a way of working that makes it dead easy to take full advantage of your inspired moments. They never hit at a convenient time, nor do they last long.

Conversely, neither should you fret too much about "writer's block," "artist's block," or whatever. If you're looking at a blank piece of paper and nothing comes to you, then go do something else. Writer's block is just a symptom of feeling like you have nothing to say, combined with the rather weird idea that you *should* feel the need to say something.

Why? If you have something to say, then say it. If not, enjoy the silence while it lasts. The noise will return soon enough. In the meantime, you're better off going out into the big, wide world, having some adventures and refilling your well. Trying to create when you don't feel like it is like making conversation for the sake of making conversation. It's not really connecting, it's just droning on like an old, drunken barfly.

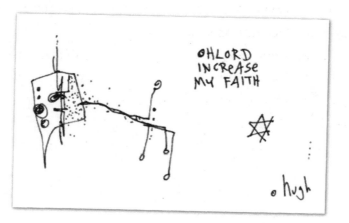

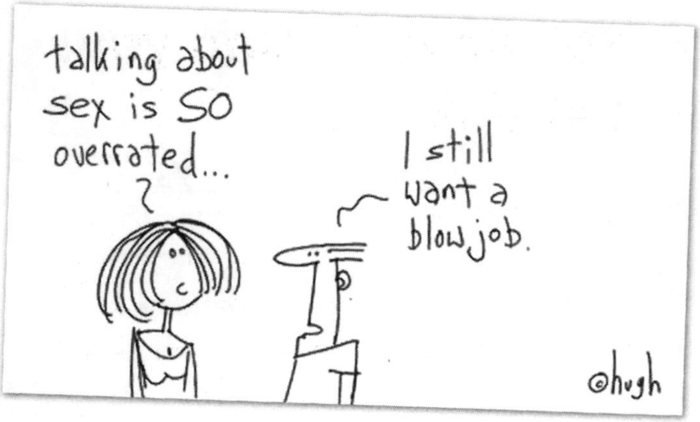
talking about sex is SO overrated...
I still want a blowjob.
©hugh

26. **You have to find your own shtick.**

A Picasso always looks like Picasso painted it. Hemingway always sounds like Hemingway. A Beethoven symphony always sounds like a Beethoven symphony. Part of being a master is learning how to sing in nobody else's voice but your own.

EVERY ARTIST IS LOOKING FOR THEIR BIG, definitive "Ah-Ha!" moment, whether they're a master or not.

That moment where they finally find their true voice, once and for all.

For me, it was when I discovered drawing on the backs of business cards.

Other, more famous, and far more notable examples would be Jackson Pollock discovering splatter paint. Or Robert Ryman discovering all-white canvases. Andy Warhol discovering silk-screen. Hunter S. Thompson discovering gonzo journalism. Duchamp discovering the found object. Jasper Johns discovering the American flag. Hemingway discovering brevity. James Joyce discovering stream-of-consciousness prose.

Was it luck? Perhaps a little bit.

But it wasn't the format that made the art great. It was the fact that somehow while playing around with something new, suddenly they found they were able to put their entire selves into it.

Only then did it become their "shtick," their true voice, etc.

That's what people responded to. The humanity, not the form. The voice, not the form.

Put your whole self into it, and you will find your true voice. Hold back and you won't. It's that simple.

You plant some
Apple Seeds.
Two weeks later
the Client says,
"Where's my
fucking Apples, Asshole?"

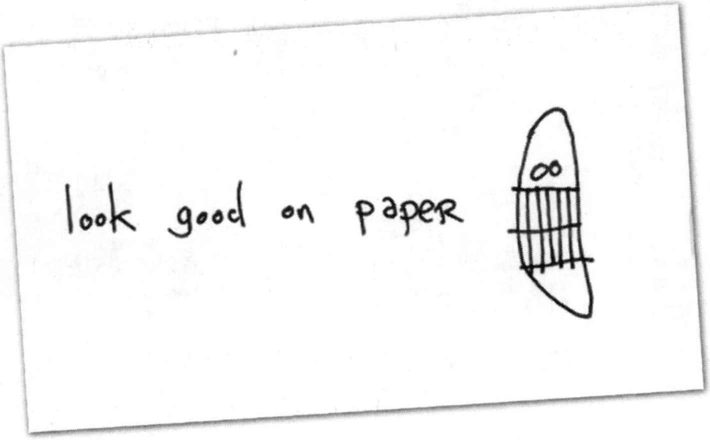
look good on paper

27. **Write from the heart.**

There is no silver bullet. There is only the love God gave you.

AS A PROFESSIONAL WRITER, I AM INTERESTED in how conversation scales.

How communication scales, *x to the power of n*, etc. etc.

Ideally, if you're in the communication business, you want to say the same thing, the same way, to an audience of millions that you would to an audience of one. Imagine the power you'd have if you could pull it off.

But sadly, it doesn't work that way.

You can't love a crowd the same way you can love a person.

And a crowd can't love you the way a single person can love you.

Intimacy doesn't scale. Not really. Intimacy is a one-on-one phenomenon.

It's not a big deal. Whether you're writing to an audience of one, five, a thousand, a million, ten million, there's really only one way to truly connect. One way that actually works:

Write from the heart.

There is no silver bullet. There is only the love God gave you.

he upgraded his conversation by inserting the name of a trendy neighborhood every third sentence.

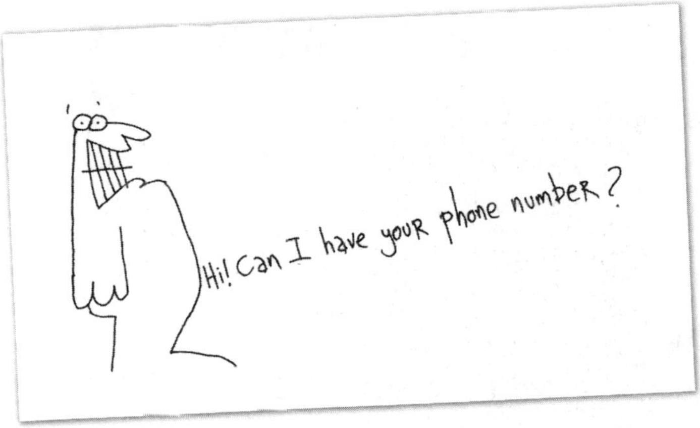
Hi! Can I have your phone number?

28. **The best way to get approval is not to need it.**

This is equally true in art and business. And love. And sex. And just about everything else worth having.

ABOUT TWENTY YEARS AGO I WAS HANGING out in the offices of *Punch*, the famous London humor magazine. I was just a kid at the time, but for some reason the cartoon editor (who was a famous cartoonist in his own right) was tolerating having me around that day.

I was asking him questions about the biz. He was answering them as best he could while he sorted through a large stack of mail.

"Take a look at this, sunshine," he said, handing a piece of paper over to me.

I gave it a look. Some long-established cartoonist whose name I recognized had written him a rather sad and desperate letter, begging to be published.

"Another whiny letter from another whiny cartoonist who used to be famous twenty-five years ago," he said, rolling his eyeballs. "I get at least fifty of them a week from other whiny formerly famous cartoonists."

He paused. Then he flashed a wicked grin.

"How *not* to get published," he said. "Write me a bloody letter like that one."

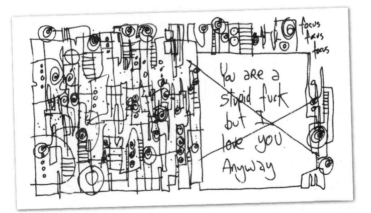

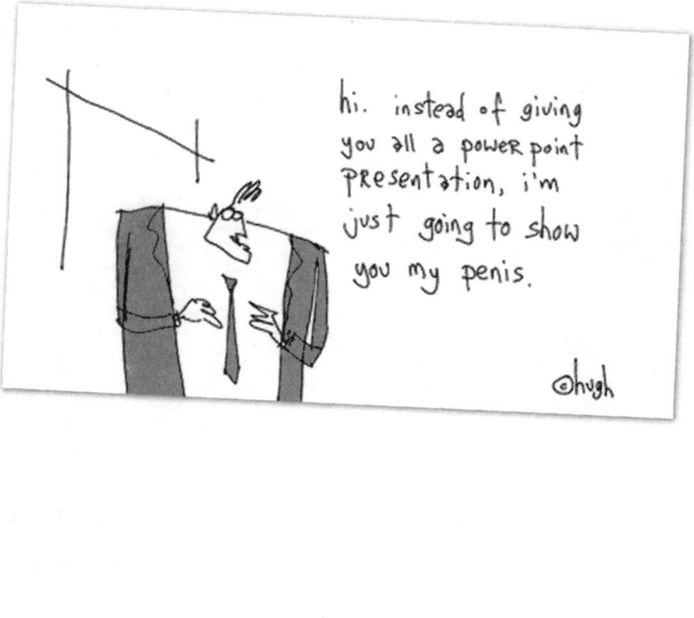
hi. instead of giving you all a power point presentation, i'm just going to show you my penis.
©hugh

29. **Power is never given. Power is taken.**

People who are "ready" give off a different vibe
from people who aren't. Animals can smell fear.
And the lack thereof.

THE MINUTE YOU BECOME READY IS THE MIN-
ute you stop dreaming. Suddenly it's no longer about "becoming." Suddenly it's about "doing."

You don't get the dream job because you walk into the editor's office for the first time and go, "Hi, I would really love to be
a sportswriter one day, please."

You get the job because you walk into the editor's office and
go, "Hi, I'm the best frickin' sportswriter on the planet." And
somehow the editor can tell you aren't lying, either.

You didn't go in there, asking the editor to give you power.

You went in there and politely informed the editor that you already have the power. That's what being "ready" means. That's what "taking power" means.

Not needing anything from another person in order to be the best in the world.

the future belongs
to the geeks.
nobody else wants it.

©hugh

Stay ahead of the
culture by
creating the culture.

©hugh

30. Whatever choice you make, the Devil gets his due eventually.

Selling out to Hollywood comes with a price. So does not selling out. Either way, you pay in full, and yes, it invariably hurts like hell.

PEOPLE ARE FOND OF SPOUTING OUT THE OLD cliché about how Van Gogh never sold a painting in his lifetime. Somehow his example serves to justify to us, decades later, that there is merit in utter failure.

Perhaps, but the man did commit suicide. The market for his work took off big-time shortly after his death. Had he decided to stick around another few decades he most likely would've entered old age quite prosperous. And sadly for failures everywhere, the cliché would have lost a lot of its power.

The fact is, the old clichés work for us in abstract terms, but they never work out in real life quite the same way. Life is messy; clichés are clean and tidy.

Of course, there is no one "true way" to make it as an artist, writer, filmmaker, or whatever it is your dream to be. Whether you follow the example of fame-and-glamour Warhol or poor-and-miserable Van Gogh doesn't matter in absolute terms.

Either extreme may raise you to the highest heights or utterly destroy you. I don't know the answer, nor does anybody else. Nobody but you and God know why you were put on this earth, and even then . . .

So when a young person asks me whether it's better to sell out or stick to one's guns, I never know what to answer. Warhol sold out shamelessly after 1968 (the year he was wounded by the gunshot of a would-be assassin) and did OK by it. I know some great artists who stuck to their guns, and all it did was make them seem more and more pathetic.

Anyone can be an idealist. Anyone can be a cynic. The hard part lies somewhere in the middle—that is, being human.

it's not what
the software does.
it's what the
user does.

@hugh

ideal working conditions:

1. life in total meltdown
2. dRink pRoblem kicking in

© hugh '07

31. The hardest part of being creative is getting used to it.

If you have the creative urge, it isn't going to go away. But sometimes it takes a while before you accept the fact.

BACK IN 1989, I WAS LIVING IN WEST LONDON, house-sitting a family member's lovely little flat over the summer. In the flat above lived the film director Tim Burton, who was in town for a couple of months while he was filming *Batman: The Movie*.

We got to know each other on and off quite well that year. We weren't that close or anything, but we saw each other around a lot. He was a pretty good neighbor, I tried to be the same.

At the time I was in my last year of college, studying to go into advertising as a copywriter. One night he and his wife came over for dinner.

Somewhere along the line the subject of my career choice came up. Back then I was a bit apprehensive about doing the "creative" thing for a living . . . in my family people always had "real" jobs in corporations and banks, etc., and the idea of breaking with tradition made me pretty nervous.

"Well," said Tim, "if you have the creative bug, it isn't ever going to go away. I'd just get used to the idea of dealing with it."

It was damn good advice. It still is.

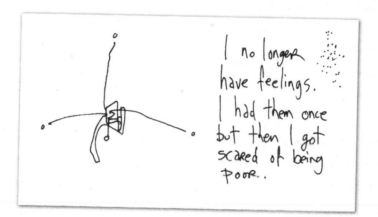

I no longer have feelings. I had them once but then I got scared of being poor.

the good news is,
they're hyper-connected.
the bad news is,
that's all they are.

©hugh

32. **Remain frugal.**

The less you can live on, the more chance your idea will succeed. This is true even after you've "made it."

IN 1997, I LANDED THE DREAM JOB. HIGH-PAID advertising copywriter. Big office. Big apartment in New York. Glamorous parties and glamorous backdrop. All feeding the urban sophisticate narrative, etc. All good.

The trouble was, even though I was being paid very well, I was still broke by the end of the month. Life in New York was expensive, and I was determined to experience it fully. I sure as hell wasn't saving anything.

Like they say, education is expensive. And I ended up paying top dollar.

Because of course, one day the recession hit, the job dried

up, and I nearly found myself on the street. Had I lived a bit more modestly I would have been able to weather the storm better.

There are a lot of people out there who, like me back in New York, make a lot of money, but spend it just as quickly. The older you get, the less you envy them. Sure, they get to go to the fancy restaurants five days a week, but they pay heavily for the privilege. They can't afford to tell their bosses to go take a hike. They can't afford to not panic when business slows down for a month or two.

Part of being creative is learning how to protect your freedom. That includes freedom from avarice.

Nobody moves to New York just in order to survive .... of course, that's what most of them end up doing......

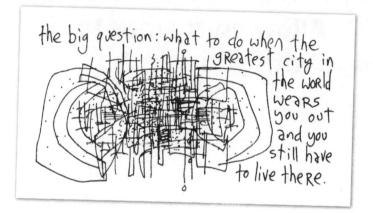

the big question: what to do when the greatest city in the world wears you out and you still have to live there.

33. **Allow your work to age with you.**

You become older faster than you think.
Be ready for it when it happens.

I HAVE A FRIEND. CALL HIM DAN.

When I first met Dan, he was a twenty-nine-year-old aspiring filmmaker, living in a one-bedroom apartment down on New York's Lower East Side, who liked to spend too much time in bars.

The last time I saw him, he was a forty-one-year-old aspiring filmmaker, living in a one-bedroom apartment down on New York's Lower East Side, who likes to spend too much time in bars.

There's a famous old quip: "A lot of people in business say they have twenty years' experience, when in fact all they really have is one year's experience, repeated twenty times."

It's not just guys in business who fall into this trap, unfortunately. It happens just as often to people taking a less conventional path. It's sad enough when you see it happen to a friend of yours. When it happens to you, it's even worse.

The good news is, it's easy enough to avoid. Especially with experience. Suddenly you realize that you're just not into the same things you once were. You used to be into staying up all night, going to parties, and now you'd rather stay in and read a book. Sure, it sounds boring, but hey, sometimes "boring" can be a lot of fun. Especially if it's on your own terms.

Just go with the flow and don't worry about it. *Especially* don't worry about the people who *are* worrying about it. They'll just slow you down.

you've only been
dead a few hours
and already
nobody cares

@hugh

127

Why do they call it "Snatch"?
'Coz there aint no honest way to get it.

34. **Being Poor Sucks.**

The biggest mistake young people make is underestimating how competitive the world is out there.

EVERYONE WILL HAVE HAD A GROUP OF FRIENDS who went hitchhiking around Europe when they were nineteen, living off ten dollars a day. And they were so happy! And they had so much fun! And money wasn't an issue!

Ha. That was Youth, that was not Reality. Reality is much bigger than Youth. And not as nice.

That's not to say cash is the be-all and end-all. But to deny the importance of the material world around you (and its hard currencies) is to detach yourself from reality. And the world *will* punish you hard, eventually, for that.

I've often been asked by young people, which do I think is a better career choice: "Creativity" or "Money"? I say both are the wrong answer. The best thing to be in this world is an effective human being. Sometimes that requires money, sometimes it doesn't. Be ready for either when it happens.

I let Jesus into my heart.
Now the bastard won't
fucking leave.

35. **Beware of turning hobbies into jobs.**

It sounds great, but there is a downside.

THE LATE BRITISH BILLIONAIRE JAMES GOLD-smith once quipped, "When a man marries his mistress, he immediately creates a vacancy."

What's true in philanderers is also true in life.

When I was about nineteen I knew this guy called Andrew, who was a junior accountant, a few years out of college.

Andrew didn't really like being an accountant—at least, that's what he was fond of saying. His passion, of all things, was antique silverware. In particular, antique silver cutlery. In particular, antique silver teaspoons.

He knew *a lot* about antique silver teaspoons. He collected them en masse. He lived and breathed them. OK, maybe that's a pretty strange hobby, but hey, he was pretty much a national authority on them.

To make a long story short, eventually he quit his accountancy gig and got a new job at a very prestigious auction house, specializing in valuing silverware.

I remember buying him a drink and congratulating him. What happy news!

A few years later, I was hanging out at the same bar with some mutual acquaintances, and his name came up in conversation. This time the news wasn't so happy.

Apparently he had recently lost his job. Apparently he had developed a huge drinking problem.

What a bloody shame.

"That's why you should never turn your hobby into your job," said one of my friends, someone far older and wiser than I. "Before, this man had a job and a hobby. Now suddenly, he's just got the job, but no hobby anymore. But a man needs both, you see. And now what does this man, who's always had a hobby, do with his time?"

My friend held up his glass.

"Answer: Drink."

Make of that what you will.

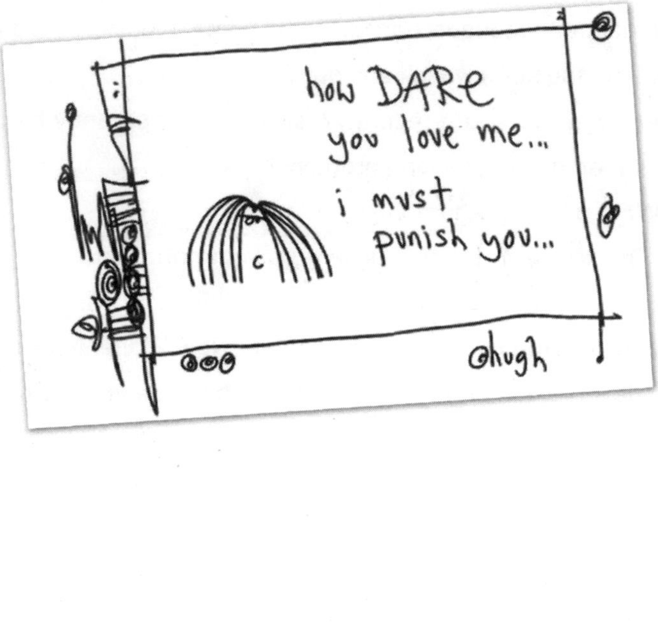
how DARE
you love me...
i must
punish you...
©hugh

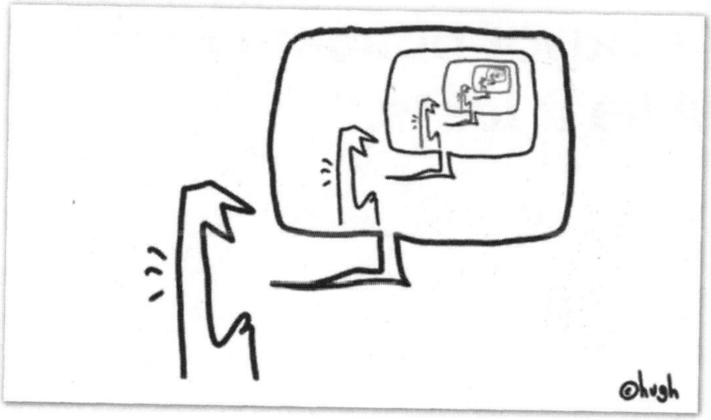
©hugh

36. **Savor obscurity while it lasts.**

Once you "make it," your work is never the same.

IT'S A FAMILIAR STORY, RETOLD COUNTLESS times. A talented person creates something amazing and wonderful when she's young, poor, hungry, and alone, and the world doesn't care. Then one day something happens and her luck is changed forever. Next thing you know she's some sort of celebrity, making all sorts of obscene sums, hanging out with royalty and movie stars. It's a dream a lot of young artists have, something to sustain them during their early, lean years.

The funny thing is, when you hear the "rock stars" talk about their climb to the top, the part they invariably speak most fondly of is not the part with all the fame, money, and parties. It's the part *before* they made it, back when they were living in a basement without electricity and "eating dog food," back when they were doing their breakthrough work.

Back when they were young, and inventing a new language to speak to the world with. More important, back when they were young, and inventing *a new language other people could also speak* to the world with.

Some years ago, after he'd been playing stadiums for a while, the rock singer Neil Young was booed off the stage by his fans when he tried playing new country-and-western material. They didn't want to share in his new adventures. No, they had paid their money to hear the classic rock, dammit. "Down by the River" and "Heart of Gold," dammit. And if they didn't get it, dammit, they'd be out for blood. As events proved.

It's hard to invent a new language when a lot of people are already heavily invested in your work (including yourself). When a lot of people are already fluent in the language you're currently speaking, and they don't want anything new from you. Like the Neil Young fans, they don't want to see your metaphorical new movie, they just want to watch the sequel to the old one.

And success needs lots of people to keep the show on the road. When it's just you, a dream, and a few cans of dog food, there's only one person to worry about. But when the dream turns into reality, there's all sorts of other people suddenly needing to be taken care of, in order to keep the engine running. Publishers, investors, managers, journalists, retailers, suppliers, groupies, employees, accountants, family members . . . and the paying customers. They all have a stake in your act, and they all want a piece of the action.

So you crank out another sequel and wait for the money to roll in. It's a living.

Of course, one reason the rock stars can speak of their basement-and-dog-food era so fondly is because it eventually came to an end; it didn't last forever. And with all the world tours and parties, this era of creating their seminal work soon became a distant memory. So quite naturally, they miss it. But if they were still "eating dog food" after a few decades, I doubt if they'd be waxing so lyrically.

But as long as you can progress from it eventually, it's a time to be savored. A time when your work is still new to you, a time when the world doesn't need to be fed, like a voracious animal.

Henry couldn't decide what he missed the most — the alcohol or the being an Asshole.

x: complete asshole
y: fucking asshole
z: complete fucking asshole

37. **Start blogging.**

The ease with which a blog (or whatever social medium you prefer) can circumvent the gatekeepers is staggering.

HOW TO GET PUBLISHED IN FRANCE

I have a friend in Paris. Call her Marie. She's a lovely woman, très chic, very smart and sexy, with a cute apartment in the Twentieth Arrondissement and a respectable job in an advertising agency. A couple of years ago, she wrote a book. A novel. In French. Lots of sex and introspection (sex and introspection being a very popular French literary combo, of course). Anyway, Marie wants to get the book published.

The last time I dined with her in Paris, Marie was telling me her tale of woe. She had spent many long months schlepping around town, trying in vain to find a publisher, which in Paris means trying to ingratiate oneself with the Parisian literary social scene. This is something that's actually quite hard to break into, given the huge numbers of unpublished sex-and-introspection novels already making the rounds. One guy, an editor at some small imprint nobody outside of Paris has ever heard of, offered to help her, but eventually gave up once he figured out that she wasn't going to sleep with him. You get the picture.

Being an avid blogger, of course, I was not very helpful.

"Your book has thirteen chapters," I say. "Voilà! That's thirteen blog posts. One chapter per blog post. Put it online, and you'll have a book offer within six months. Trust me."

Of course, this is not how you do it in Paris, supposedly. You do it by going to all the right parties and hobnobbing with all the right people, supposedly. If you're good at it, you get a book deal, supposedly. If you're really good at it, they'll also let you go on the highbrow TV talk show circuit and pontificate about "Culture" with all the other erudite culture vultures, supposedly. Maybe give you an occasional column in *Le Figaro*, supposedly. An intoxicating combo of both intellectual celebrity and bourgeois respectability, supposedly. Very elite, supposedly. Very French, supposedly.

Sadly, she never went with the blog option. Sure, it could've worked quite easily (hey, it worked easily enough for Tom Reynolds, the London ambulance driver who got a book deal based on his blog writings), but doing that would probably have been seen as a bit *gauche* by the other groovy cats in the Parisian literary scene. And I suspect she wanted membership in that club, every bit as much as she wanted to see her name in print.

Of course, as anybody who listens to NPR or the BBC will know, we have similar culturally elite hierarchies here in the English-speaking world, just maybe not so hardcore. There's something strangely curious about how the idea of "The Novel," *Le Roman*, has such a strong hold on the French imagination; there's something so heroic to them about the idea of the *Auteur* that it's hard to explain to people from more philistine parts of the world. On one level, you can easily admire such a strong reverence for a classic art form. On another level, such attachment can needlessly hold you back.

Whatever. If I were Marie, I would still reconsider blogging the book in full. And I would post up an English version as well, to give the book the greatest chance of being read by people outside her French, urban microcosm. Sure, the Parisian literary purists will bitch and moan, but hey, they're Parisian literary purists—they're going to bitch and moan anyway.

It certainly worked for me. As I said in the preface, this book you're now reading started life out as a 13,000-word essay on my blog, gapingvoid.com. It was downloaded and read about a million times, then the next thing you know publishers started approaching me. Happy Ending.

And of course, I wouldn't limit this advice just to writers. If I were a painter, I wouldn't move to New York and wait tables for ten years, trying to find an art gallery to represent me. I would just post the paintings online, build up a large enough audience, and *eventually* the sales will come.

And I wouldn't stop there, either. The fact that you're reading this probably means that you're in a line of work that is idea-driven, be it IT, law, accounting, whatever. So put some of your ideas on a blog and get them "out there." Eventually the fish will start biting. Just remember that it doesn't happen overnight. It usually takes a couple of years of continual posting to build up enough trust to where people are willing to invest in you financially. But you never know. It could be a couple of months, it could take a couple of years. But it certainly beats a decade waiting tables in Manhattan.

the short
tail

the
pile
of
bodies

38. **Meaning scales, people don't.**

From my blog entry "Meaning Scales," February 2005:

> As Buddha says, there is no one road to Nirvana. Enlighten-
> ment is a house with 6 billion doors. While we're alive, we
> intend not to find THE DOOR, not A DOOR, but to find OUR
> OWN, UNIQUE DOOR.
>
> And we're willing to pay for the privilege. We're willing to
> give up money and time and power and sex and status and
> certainty and comfort in order to find it.
>
> And guess what? It'll be a great door. It'll add to this life.
> It'll resonate. Not just with us, but with everybody it comes in
> contact with. The door will be useful and productive. Alive
> and kicking. It'll create wealth and laughter and joy. It'll pull
> its own weight, it'll give back to others. It'll be centered on

compassion, but will also be intolerant of dullards, parasites and cynics.

It may be modest, it may not. It could be a little candle shop; it could be a software company with the GNP of Sweden. It could involve politics or working with the elderly. It could be starting a design studio or opening a bar with Cousin Mike. It could be a screenplay, oil paints, or discovering the violin. It doesn't matter. *Meaning Scales.*

Sure, I was pretty drunk on the Kool-Aid when I wrote that, but I think the main point is still valid. The size of the endeavor doesn't matter as much as how meaningful it becomes to you.

But given a choice between two paths, both valid, how do you know which one to take? How do you know which one has the meaningful payoff?

The answer, of course, is that you don't. Whether we're talking about moving to New York to become an "Art Star," or opening up a humble coffee shop in Alpine, Texas, that's why they're called "adventures." Because you don't know how it's going to end.

All you can do is admit to yourself that yes, this is an adventure, and to accept it as such, surprises and all. With a little bit of practice you eventually get into the flow of it.

Yes, anything worth doing takes lots of practice. Adventures included.

And when I say "People don't scale," I'm stating the obvious:

that no matter how meteoric your rise to the top [or not], you are still as beholden to the day-to-day realities as any living creature.

Birth, sickness, death, falling in love, watching TV, raising families, mowing the lawn, going to the movies, taking your nephew to a ball game, drinking beer, hanging out with your buddies, playing Frisbee on the beach, painting the house, tending the garden. No matter where your adventure takes you, most of what is truly meaningful is still to be found revolving around the mundane stuff you did before you embarked on your adventure. The stuff that'll still be going on long after you and I are both dead, long after our contribution to the world is forgotten.

But often, one needs to have that big adventure before truly appreciating how utterly wonderful all that simple, mundane stuff actually is. Going full circle.

this city is killing me but what a glorious death it is

3 LITTLE WORDS
(in descending
  order of
  importance) $\longrightarrow$

LOVE
you.

39. **When your dreams become reality, they are no longer your dreams.**

If you are successful, it'll never come from the direction you predicted. Same is true if you fail.

A BRIEF HISTORY OF THE "CARTOONS DRAWN ON THE BACKS OF BUSINESS CARDS" FORMAT

As this book reaches its end, I'm thinking how it's been *over ten years* since I first came up with the "cartoons drawn on the backs of business cards" format. And it seems like *I've only just* got them to the commercially successful level I thought they were capable of reaching.

Better late than never, I suppose.

A friend asked me recently, had I known it would take this

long, would I have bothered in the first place? I have in my mind this fantasy version of myself that makes reasonable and sensible decisions, more often than not. This reasonable and sensible person, if he existed, would probably have answered, "No. Definitely not."

But none of this is sensible. None of it ever was. So yeah, knowing what I know now, I probably wouldn't have behaved any differently. I'm not proud of that; I'm not ashamed, either. It just is.

Was it worth the cost? Not really. It never is. Van Gogh once told his brother, "No painting ever sells for as much as it cost the artist to make it." I've yet to meet in the flesh any artist who could prove him wrong.

Though looking on the bright side, it *is* nice after years of struggling away in obscurity to have a body of work that you're actually proud of, one that (a) makes you a good living, (b) exceeds your earlier expectations of what you thought you were capable of achieving as a human being, and perhaps most important, (c) has given a lot of other people a lot of joy and value.

When I was a kid in college, there were very few avenues a cartoonist could take, if she wished to be successful. There was no Internet back then. There were only newspapers, magazines, books, TV, movies, comic books, merchandising, and little else. A world I find hard to imagine now. And besides, I never saw my work as particularly commercial, so even if I did give it my best shot, I never thought it would ever realistically pay off.

So in my last year of college, feigning maturity, I turned my attention to landing a job that would pay my bills upon graduation. From what I could then tell, writing TV commercials seemed to use the same part of the brain it took to draw cartoons, and I wasn't a bad cartoonist, so I decided to give Madison Avenue a go. It looked like it could be interesting.

Somehow I managed to get a job as an advertising copywriter, straight out of school. Some skill was needed, most of it was luck, but when you're in your early twenties and entering the serious job market for the first time, you'll take whatever you can get.

Though I was in the ad industry off-and-on for over a decade, I don't think about it too much, now. Some part of me has blacked it out. Besides being *very* hard work, it wasn't much fun. I was very much in the ranks of what I would call the "In-Betweenies"— that is, those good enough to get and keep a pretty well-paid position in an ad agency, but not good enough to really get ahead in it; not good enough to enjoy it properly. This was the world I lived in, in 1998 New York, when I started drawing the cartoons with a vengeance. And like every other In-Betweenie my age, it was a tiring, stressful time for me.

And then the Internet happened. . . .

Over the next couple of years, yes, I drew a lot of cartoons, but I didn't do much with them. They were just a hobby. Besides, I had a lot going on at the time, with the job and the New York lifestyle to maintain. Most of my cartoon audience back then consisted of fellow New York barflies that I had foisted them upon.

But all good things must come to an end. One day I found myself underemployed, broke, and pissed off with life in general. With nothing better to do besides waiting for the phone to ring, in May 2001 I started my blog, gapingvoid.com.

I would like to say that the Web site took off soon after, the cartoons were a smash hit, and things improved dramatically right away, but sadly that didn't happen. I just kept at it, day after day, building it up slowly. That's still how it happens, for the most part.

The million-dollar contract has yet to arrive in the mail. That's OK; somewhere along the line I figured out how to make good money off them, *indirectly.*

How? It's pretty straightforward, in retrospect. I posted the cartoons online, and because I had a lot of free time on my hands, I then spent a long time tracking what happened to them, once they went out into the ether. This was 2002, just as blogs were beginning to hit the scene. This was the beginning of Google's rise to the top of the search market. This was the heyday of Technorati.com, when people wanted to start seeing what was happening on the Web *right now,* not just historically.

Over the next year or two watching the cartoons traveling about, watching what other bloggers were up to, I started getting a pretty good feel for how the Internet *actually* worked, not just how the journalists and marketing folk told people it worked.

After a while I started posting my thoughts about this brave new world online. And after a while people started e-mailing me, offering to pay me good money if I would share more of what I had learned online with them.

Sharing this information for me was *a lot more fun* and better paid than trying to sell ads to clients, so hey, I went for it.

So far I've managed to turn it into a pretty nice business. A lot more money, for a lot less stress and time than Madison Avenue ever offered me. Not a bad outcome.

The thing is, none of it happened on purpose. It just kinda sorta happened, one random event at a time.

I find having two strings to my bow, cartoons and Internet, helps the business out a lot. I like to play them off each other. Sorry, I can't draw you a cartoon; I'm too busy doing Internet stuff. Sorry, I can't help you with your Internet problem; I'm too busy drawing something for a client. I totally believe that if I gave one of them up for good, the other one would crash and burn overnight. It's maintaining the creative tension between the two, an extension of the aforementioned "Sex & Cash Theory," which keeps things interesting. For both me and the good folk paying my bills.

I never intended to be a professional cartoonist. I never intended to become an Internet jockey. But somehow the two got mashed up to create this third thing. That's what I mean by "If you are successful, it'll never come from the direction you predicted."

It's good to be young and full of dreams. Dreams of one day doing something "insanely great." Dreams of love, beauty, achievement, and contribution. But understand they have a life of their own, and they're not very good at following instructions. Love them, revere them, nurture them, respect them, but don't ever become a slave to them. Otherwise you'll kill them off prematurely, before they get the chance to come true.

Good luck.

We need
to talk.
After that,
you need
to shut up.

40. **None of this is rocket science.**

If I had to condense this entire book into a line or two, it would read something like, "Work hard. Keep at it. Live simply and quietly. Remain humble. Stay positive. Create your own luck. Be nice. Be polite."

I HOPE SOME OF THIS WAS HELPFUL. HOPE YOU find what you're looking for. Thanks for reading. Godspeed. Seriously. Rock on.

enRich
simplify
©hugh

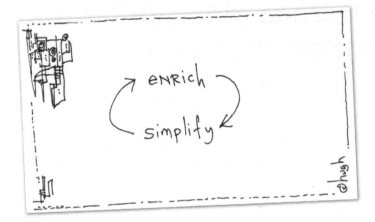

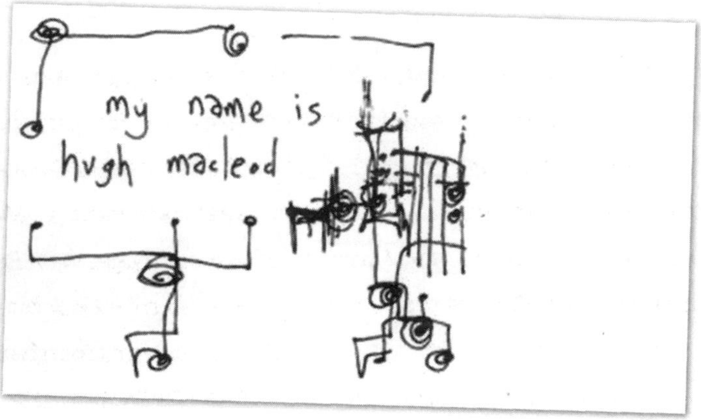
my name is
hugh macleod

Acknowledgments

My sister, Sarah, who always loved me, even in tough times. My mother and father, who taught me how to take a risk. My grandparents, who taught me the importance of character. Mark O'Donnell, who inspired me from an early age. My third grade teacher, Miss Lucity, who encouraged me from an equally early age. Nick Barbaro and Louis Black at the *Austin Chronicle,* who first published my cartoons. Jonathan Gillard, who taught me how to make a living. Jeffrey and Jillian, who edited this book. Seth Godin, who always helped me along the way, including introducing me to Jeffrey and Jillian. My agent, Lisa DiMona, who rocks. The thousands of bloggers who have inspired me over the years—especially Jeff Jarvis, Doc Searls, Fred Wilson, Jerry Colonna, Rick Segal, Steve Clayton, Joi Ito, Lee Thomas, Clay Shirky, Loren Feldman, Thomas Mahon, Kathy Sierra, Robert Scoble, Mike Arrington, Loic Le Meur, David Brain, and JP Rangaswami. And last, a special note of thanks to my business partner, Jason Korman—he knows why.